THE CAUSES OF
THE WAR OF 1812

THE CAUSES OF THE WAR OF 1812

National Honor or National Interest?

Edited by **BRADFORD PERKINS**

University of Michigan

KRIEGER PUBLISHING COMPANY
MALABAR, FLORIDA

Original Edition   1962
Reprint Edition   1976, 1983

Printed and Published by
KRIEGER PUBLISHING COMPANY
KRIEGER DRIVE
MALABAR, FLORIDA 32950

Printed in the United States of America

Library of Congress Cataloging in Publication Data

Perkins, Bradford, 1925-   ed.
    The causes of the War of 1812.

    Reprint of the 1966 issue of the ed. first published
in 1962 by Holt, Rinehart and Winston, New York, in
series: American problem studies.
    Bibliography: p.
    SUMMARY: Varied interpretations by leading authorities
of the mixed motives and complex causes of the War of 1812
and the diplomacy that proceded it.
    1. United States—History—War of 1812—Causes—
Addresses, essays, lectures. [1. United States—History
—War of 1812—Causes—Addresses, essays, lectures]
I. Title.
[E357.P64   1976]   973.5'21   76-3657
ISBN 0-88275-408-4

10   9   8   7   6   5   4   3

CONTENTS

INTRODUCTION

Quite justly, the War of 1812 is often called "the second war for independence." Although the United States gained formal recognition of its freedom in 1783, for many years after that date the new nation remained a very minor factor in international politics, and the major powers of Europe felt free to treat the Americans as though that independence were not complete. The declaration of war in June 1812, most historians agree, was the product of resentment at various British actions that in effect challenged American sovereignty, on the sea or on the land. Even if, as some maintain, many war hawks, the prowar legislators of the day, wanted war because it would make possible conquests in British Canada or in Spanish Florida, an inevitable consequence of this expansion would have been, by strengthening the power of the United States, to strengthen its freedom of action. Certainly the War of 1812 marked an important step toward the development of the American nation as an independent power with the strength and the will to make its voice heard.

To call this conflict a "second war for independence" is, however, not enough. Why, precisely, did diplomacy break down and war come about? What forces and what leaders were responsible? These questions, so frequently asked about all wars, challenge the diplomatic historian. Since, as is the case with most historical developments, more than one "cause" must be taken into account, almost infinite variations of emphasis are always possible. The coming of the War of 1812, like the origins of the three wars in which the United States has engaged since 1898 — and even the causes of the internal conflicts of 1775 and 1861 — has evoked sharply contrasting explanations.

In a negative sense, war came in 1812 because an alternative policy failed. Although he was no doctrinaire pacifist but a man ready to fight when "peace becomes more losing than war," Thomas Jefferson cherished peace. Down to 1812 he, his successor, James Madison, and their Republic party sought to vindicate American demands by the use of economic weapons. In 1807 they imposed an embargo upon American shipping and exports. In 1809, driven from this experiment by opposition at home, they fell back upon the Non-

1

intercourse Act, which prohibited — but was actually ineffective to prevent — commerce with both England and France. The next year, retreating a step farther, the Republicans passed Macon's Bill No. 2, reopening commerce but promising, if one of the great belligerents ceased to violate American commerce, to close trade with the opponent of that power. In the summer of 1810, Napoleon announced the repeal of his restrictions on American trade. Although his pledge was insincere and at best partly observed, the United States responded by cutting off all imports from Great Britain. Ultimately this action and other pressures compelled England to withdraw her offensive orders in council, but this was not known to the Americans in June 1812.

The failure, or at best the delayed success, of the Republican policy of economic coercion has intrigued many scholars. A few, like Louis M. Sears in his *Jefferson and the Embargo* (1927), have maintained that the embargo was an idealistic experiment, a temporary withdrawal from the arenas of conflict which at least delayed the outbreak of war. Most writers, particularly in recent years, have preferred to emphasize the long Republican devotion to the idea of economic coercion as a powerful aggressive weapon of diplomacy. They have therefore investigated the failure of this policy, seeking to explain the political revolution against it, the degree of success that marked its enforcement, and the reasons why the British economy proved less vulnerable than Jefferson and Madison hoped. In selections that follow, Leonard D. White and Herbert Heaton consider these problems.

Still, since the embargo and its successors were essentially a reaction against European insult, to explain their failure does not fully answer the question of war causation. More fundamental sources of conflict must be sought among the pressures and events that inspired both the embargo and the later, more positive policy of armed resistance. In the nineteenth century, American historians emphasized the complaints stressed in James Madison's war message and the debates of the war-hawk Congress. Their viewpoint has come to be called the maritime interpretation, since it stressed British violations of American rights upon the high seas. Among those who most forcefully expressed this thesis were John Bach McMaster, the engineer-turned-historian whose *History of the American People* appeared between 1883 and 1913, and Alfred Thayer Mahan, naval officer and philosopher of sea power, whose *Sea Power in Its Relations to the War of 1812* was published in 1905.

The maritime interpretation stresses the impressment of American seamen, the orders in council interrupting American trade on the high seas, and the unprecedentedly broad blockade of enemy ports carried out by the Royal Navy. Impressment deprived the American marine of much needed seamen and undermined the honor of the young nation by showing that its flag could not protect those who served under it. Almost from the beginning of independence, at least since 1790, American statesmen protested against impressment, although at first they emphasized the kidnapping of American citizens rather than the basic problem, the forcible removal of mariners of whatever nationality from the decks of American ships. Jefferson rejected a treaty negotiated at London in 1806 by James Monroe and William Pinkney primarily because it did not contain a British promise to end impressment, and in 1807, taking advantage of the national outcry produced by the attack upon U.S.S. *Chesapeake,* he again unsuccessfully attempted to force England to give up her traditional policy. Thereafter impressment remained a nagging wound, and particularly in the closing weeks of the war-hawk Congress, it was pushed forward as a major ground of complaint against Great Britain.

Ships and cargoes, as well as seamen, fell prey to the British. The dispute concerning these seizures was almost as old, as a matter of fact, as the controversy over impressment, for it went back to the early days of the Franco-British war begun in 1793. For more than a decade British policy fluctuated, and America chose to tolerate seizures that were not numerous enough to prevent a great commercial boom. Then, in 1805, Britain stepped up the pressure. James Stephen's famous pamphlet, arguing that neutral commerce was, to borrow his title, *War in Disguise,* helped to mobilize opinion against trade that, it was held, helped France and undermined England. Soon, in the case of the American ship *Essex,* Sir William Grant laid down new and harsher rules for neutrals. The next year, Monroe and Pinkney failed to procure concessions that satisfied their superiors in Washington, and the conflict of view rapidly sharpened. In November 1807, partly in response to Napoleonic action against British trade, London issued new orders in council that effectively prohibited American trade with Europe unless this trade was carried on through British entrepôts. Despite several modifications, notably in the order in council of April 1809, British policy remained essentially unchanged until the war came. American protests were ignored or rejected until the final revocation of the orders in June 1812. The anger engendered by interruption of American trade was increased by the fact that, through special licenses and other devices, Great Britain permitted her own subjects to carry on trade with Europe prohibited to the Americans. She was, in short, attempting to force her own goods onto the Continent as well as to prevent any of her commercial rivals from trading with her military enemy.

The maritime interpretation provokes certain questions. Why did the Americans not go to war earlier than they did? Impressment and the orders in council were old grievances in 1812, and as a matter of fact neither of them was as burdensome in that year as in, say, 1807 and 1808. Moreover, the American government virtually abandoned its efforts to convince England to end impressment after the failure of the Monroe-Pinkney negotiations. Why, after a period of tolerance, was this issue again brought to the fore? Then, too, both impressment and the seizure of ships most directly affected areas in the North, the home of most American seamen and ships. Why was it that the South and West, not the North, most vigorously championed war in 1812? Finally, why was it that America fought England when France dealt just as harshly with American commerce?

Such questions have led to re-examinations of the maritime interpretation but not to its abandonment. Henry Adams' famous *History* hinted at certain shortcomings in the traditional view as early as 1890, but as the selection in this pamphlet indicates, Adams still tended to give first place to these issues as a cause of war. Moreover, as Warren H. Goodman states in his valuable historiographical article, "The Origins of the War of 1812,"[1] Adams certainly did not press any alternative interpretation. As recently as 1940, in a volume which established itself as the most comprehensive survey of the coming of war, A. L. Burt stressed maritime issues, although he did also present to his readers a summary of alternative interpretations. Burt's point of view is reflected in the first selection in this pamphlet, where he describes what he apparently considers to be the most important issues between England and the United States.

Seeking to explain Western bellicosity, and sometimes also the support of the South, an increasing number of scholars have in effect turned their backs upon the seaboard. One small school, foreshadowed by Howard T. Lewis,[2] argued that Westerners coveted the rich lands of Canada and were willing to go to war to obtain them. This conclusion, independently reached, was endorsed by Louis M. Hacker a decade later, in 1924. Almost immediately it brought a vigorous rebutal from Julius W. Pratt, and since that time the "land hunger" argument has not been seriously pressed. The articles by Hacker and Pratt, however, so clearly show how historians can reach opposite conclusions from approximately the same evidence that they are reproduced in this volume.

Pratt was not content with mere negativism. Indeed, soon after criticizing Hacker, he put forward his own views in *Expansionists of 1812*. In this volume, Pratt in effect expanded upon an argument first advanced by Dice R. Anderson[3] that frontiersmen were convinced that only by driving the British from Canada could they end the flow of supplies and advice that encouraged the Indians to resist American expansion westward. The Southerners, Pratt argued, also wanted a war of conquest, with Florida as their object. The two sections accordingly formed a temporary alliance that carried the declaration of war through the Congress.

Pratt's thesis invites challenging questions. How satisfactory is a defini-

[1] *Mississippi Valley Historical Review*, vol. XXVIII (1941-1942), pp. 171-186.

[2] "A Reanalysis of the Causes of the War of 1812," *Americana*, vol. VI (1911), pp. 506-516, 577-585.

[3] "The Insurgents of 1811," American Historical Association, *Annual Report for 1911*, vol. I, pp. 165-176.

tion of the West that includes not only Kentucky and Tennessee but also the sparsely settled portions of Maine, Vermont, New Hampshire, and New York? When did fear of the Indians, and their alleged masters in Canada, first become acute? If it predates 1811 or 1812, why did this fear only then become politically vocal? Why did Pennsylvania, with scarcely any reason to fear the Indians or to desire Florida, provide sixteen prowar votes, the most of any state, in the House of Representatives? Moreover, to shift the ground somewhat, how general was the Southern desire for Florida? And what evidence supports the idea of an alliance between South and West to attain their quite different purposes? Some of these questions become less important if one remembers Pratt's caution that he was dealing "with one set of causes only." They do, however, show the dangers of too great reliance on any single causative factor and suggest serious shortcomings in the simplified version of Pratt's thesis that is found in most contemporary history textbooks.

The most recent "Western" interpretation has in a sense completed the circle, bringing us by a roundabout route back to the maritime thesis with which historians began. In 1931 George R. Taylor opened fresh, fertile ground in the article reprinted here, and he buttressed his conclusions with a second article on "Prices in the Mississippi Valley Preceding the War of 1812."[4] While Taylor did not deny the importance, to Westerners, of the Indian challenge, he suggested that a different interpretation also had to be considered. He pointed out that only portions of the West were affected by the Indian threat, whereas the entire section was dependent upon foreign trade. Westerners blamed low prices on the interruptions of exports, settled upon England as the power chiefly responsible for this interruption, and thus came to support a drive for war. Since 1931, no one has chosen to deny Taylor's hypothesis as such, although a number of students, including A. L. Burt, have asked if this thesis might not be applied to sections other than the trans-Appalachian area as well. In a recent article, included below, Margaret K. Latimer shows that a test of the Taylor thesis in South Carolina indicates that it makes sense for that area too; at the same time, she questions that portion of Pratt's argument which rests upon the proposition that all the South desired to acquire the Floridas.

Both Taylor and Mrs. Latimer clearly show the existence of a depression in 1811 and 1812. Still, one might ask, do they satisfactorily explain why a similar depression during the embargo did not bring war? Did anyone suggest that reopening trade with Britain and accepting the loss of the French market, always much smaller, would restore prosperity? Does this thesis, as Burt asks, make sense in the Middle states and the North? Why did so many Federalists challenge the view that British maritime policy was responsible for depression and falling prices?

Geographical

The de-emphasis of the West is carried further by Norman K. Risjord and Reginald Horsman in their articles in this pamphlet. Whereas it has always been assumed by those who endorsed various Western interpretations that this new, vigorous, nationalistic frontier was more attentive to the call of honor than any other section, Risjord argues that the sense of humiliation was national. He maintains that leaders from all sections complained that British actions were in fact a challenge to America's sovereignty. Thus Risjord returns to a theme stressed by the early "maritime" school, for writers like Mahan considered the orders in council and impressment important both for their direct impact and for their implications with regard to American honor. Horsman comes to much the same conclusion but adds an important thought of his own. He stresses the almost national character of the outcry for Canadian conquest, maintaining that the explanation is to be found, very simply, in the vulnerability of Canada to attack. In no other way, so Americans then believed, could they so easily strike a military blow to enhance the nation's honor.

Once again we find a proposed interpretation raising important questions. Granted that congressmen from all sections spoke of national honor, the fact remains that the representatives from the South and West spoke most often on this theme. Why was it that Northerners were less able to see the psychological implications of British policy? Did congressmen mean what they said, or did they, as politicians often do, cloak more material and selfish interests in the language of national honor? Why were insults to the nation more deeply felt in 1812, when impressments and even ship seizures were relatively few, than in 1807, when the attack upon the *Chesapeake,* surely a more obvious challenge to national sovereignty, failed to bring war? These questions suggest that, like other interpretations, the national-honor hypothesis cannot stand alone.

Clearly one of the critical factors in the decision for war was the position of James Madison. It was long accepted that the President was a weakling without ideas, dragooned into war by more bellicose members of his own party, essentially confused or peace-minded. In a recent biography that challenges this traditional view, Irving Brant argues that Madison, while no fire-eater, was ready for war and used the power of the administration to press for it in the closing months of peace. The selection from that biography reprinted here is balanced by another taken from the most recent book to survey the entire problem. In this work the editor of this pamphlet takes a position halfway between that of Brant and the traditionalists. He argues that Madison reluctantly reached the conclusion that war must come but had not the force to impose his decision on the Congress. In the concluding selection, George Dangerfield briefly analyzes the war message Madison finally sent to Congress on June 1, 1812.

Not one of the interpretations discussed above was left unmentioned, either by advocates or opponents of war, in 1811 and 1812. Congressmen and newspaper editors of all parties exhaustively discussed the orders in council. Madison's war message and *Niles' Register*, a leading Republican journal, stressed impressment. John Randolph and the Federalists attacked the Republicans for casting covetous eyes upon Canada. Representatives of the agrarian sections and leading Western newspapers, notably the *Lexington* (Ky.) *Reporter*, stressed the economic distress presumably caused by the orders in council. And the themes of national honor and presidential weakness sprang frequently to the lips of those debating the issue of war or peace. Thus, in one sense, historians have really only continued a contemporary controversy. Their disagreements, like those of the men of Madison's and Clay's time, suggest that the problem of war causation is highly complicated. Historians will certainly continue to debate the relative importance of the various explanations put forward to explain the coming of war in 1812.

CHRONOLOGY

1803 — War resumed between England and France

1805 — May 22–The *Essex* decision
October 21–The battle of Trafalgar

1806 — April 18–Nonimportation Act (application delayed until
December 14, 1807)
November 21 – Berlin Decree
December 31–Monroe-Pinkney treaty (rejected by Jefferson)

1807 — June 22–Clash between U.S.S. *Chesapeake* and H.M.S. *Leopard*
November 11–Orders in council
December 17–Milan Decree
December 22–Embargo Act

1809 — March 1–Nonintercourse Act
March 4–Inauguration of Madison
April 18-19–Erskine agreement (rejected by Great Britain)
September 30–Indian land cession by Treaty of Fort Wayne

1810 — May 1–Macon's Bill No. 2
August 5–Cadore letter

1811 — February 2–Trade with England closed
November 4–Twelfth Congress convenes
November 7–Battle of Tippecanoe

1812 — April 4–American trade embargoed
May 11–Spencer Perceval assassinated
June 1–Madison's war message
June 18–Declaration of war
June 23–Repeal of the orders in council

Congressional Voting on the Declaration of War, by States

	House of Representatives		Senate	
	For	Against	For	Against
New Hampshire	3	2	1	1
Vermont	3	1	1	0
Massachusetts (including Maine)	6	8	1	1
Rhode Island	0	2	0	2
Connecticut	0	7	0	2
New York	3	11	1	1
New Jersey	2	4	1	1
Delaware	0	1	0	2
Pennsylvania	16	2	2	0
Maryland	6	3	1	1
Virginia	14	5	2	0
North Carolina	6	3	2	0
South Carolina	8	0	2	0
Georgia	3	0	2	0
Ohio	1	0	0	1
Kentucky	5	0	1	1
Tennessee	3	0	2	0
	79	49	19	13

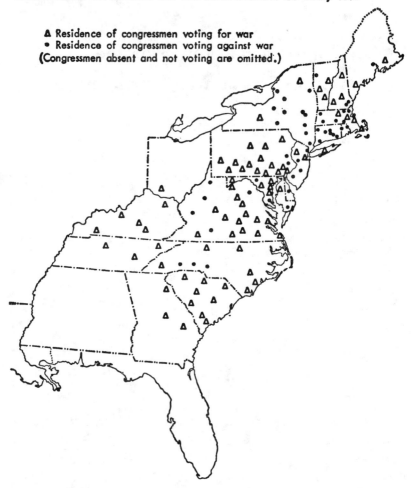

CONGRESSIONAL ACTION ON THE DECLARATION OF WAR, 1812

▲ Residence of congressmen voting for war
• Residence of congressmen voting against war
(Congressmen absent and not voting are omitted.)

From Bradford Perkins, *Prologue to War, England and the United States, 1805-1812,* Berkeley, 1961, p. 409. Reprinted with the permission of the University of California Press.

A. L. BURT, Canadian born Rhodes scholar, has spent most of his teaching career at the University of Minnesota. Although most of his other writings are on Canadian history, in the work quoted here he minimizes, though he does not ignore, the Canadian problem as a contributory factor in the coming of war. The complexity of the impressment and ship-seizure controversies is clearly shown in the following discussion.*

The Nature of the Maritime Issues

The second period of the European war, which opened with the rupture of the Peace of Amiens in May, 1803, presents a striking parallel [to that from 1793 to 1801]. Again the United States found that the equilibrium of neutrality was essentially unstable. Again the pressure from both sides was so intolerable that she sought an escape by accommodation with either, which of course meant the abandonment of neutrality. This time, however, the United States rejected the treaty negotiated by Monroe and Pinkney which, like Jay's Treaty, might have pushed France against her. This time it was a fight to the finish between the powerful belligerents. Both scorned her potential resistance and resorted to more violent measures, thereby making it more difficult for her to find any basis of accommodation with either. Neither would yield to her demands even to win her alliance, which was offered in the vain hope of playing off one against the other. She had an abundance of provocation for making war on both, but that was utterly impossible. Finally, so it has been said, Napoleon tricked her into declaring it against Britain. But we can see this end coming independently of his deception: for Britain, being in command of the sea, pressed much harder than France upon American neutral rights under international law; and France, having no foothold on the continent of North America, was much less vulnerable.

Before following in detail the evolu-

*A. L. Burt, The United States, Great Britain, and British North America from the Revolution to the Establishment of Peace after the War of 1812, New Haven, 1940, pp. 210-224, 254-255. Reprinted with the permission of the Carneigie Endowment for International Peace.

tion just outlined, it may be well to clarify the issues in the quarrel between the United States and Britain arising out of the latter's conflict with France. To accomplish this purpose, it will first be advisable to make some comments upon international law; for the quarrel was embedded in it, each side seeking to uphold its own "rights" under that law.

The nature of international law is perhaps the most important thing of all to remember in this connection. As a human institution, law implies some legislator and some tribunal capable of interpreting it and commanding its enforcement; but the sovereignty of the state has denied these conditions for international law, and therefore many careful authorities have insisted that it is not law at all. Strictly speaking, it has been a body of rules derived from common custom and consent. Private individuals, such as Grotius and Vattel, analyzed and expounded it in scholarly texts which became classics but nothing more. The principles thus set forth, being based on precedents which were by no means uniform, were necessarily very general and always open to conflicting interpretations to cover conflicting interests. Then the only solution was the superior force of one side. The whole structure was made more uncertain still by one principle, that of reprisal, which might undo any other principle, and by the insoluble problem of change. Consent is necessary for change, but consent becomes most impossible when change becomes most imperative — when war reveals new circumstances that undermine and destroy the old law governing the conduct of hostilities.

The relation between the "common law of nations" and specific treaties has also been fruitful of much trouble. Britain maintained that the former allowed her to do to the United States certain things which, under the latter, she could not do to certain European powers. The United States therefore insisted that Britain, by signing the latter, had inferentially abandoned her position under the former. Britain, on the other hand, insisted that she had inferentially strengthened it by concluding these treaties. They regulated only the relations between the signatories. By making an exception to the general rule as it applied among themselves, they confirmed its application elsewhere. The law of the world still governed the relations between Britain and America, and it would continue to do so until they agreed to change it. Finally it should not be forgotten that the law has undergone an evolution, and that the principles recognized at one time do not necessarily apply earlier or even later. The failure to recognize this evolution has often befuddled those who would explain old quarrels.

Impressment was the most baffling issue between the two countries. Though thrust forward by the war, it was not a question of the laws of war which define the balance between belligerent and neutral rights. It concerned something more permanent, more deep-seated — sovereignty. It was raised by the attraction of British seamen to the American service. They deserted the navy, where life was too much like a floating hell; and they left the British mercantile marine, whence they were liable at any time to be impressed into the navy. There was only one place where they could go, and it was an inviting heaven [sic] where they would be at home right away. The merchant marine of the United States was hungry for sailors. Under the stimulus of the war, it was expanding so rapidly that it required four or five thousand additional hands every year. The increased demand tripled American wages afloat. This salvation of the British tar, however, threatened the destruction of Britain by draining the lifeblood of her sea power, the one thing that stood between her and downfall. To check this vital loss, British warships searched American vessels and removed British fugitives.

Necessity overrides law, and Britain was impelled by necessity. But she insisted that her action was not illegal. Though this may seem strange now, it was not then, for important developments in international law and usage have since taken place. One is in our concept of nationality. We have become accustomed to think of people changing their national status almost as readily as they change their shirts. Then nationality was commonly considered to be about as impossible to change as one's skin. It is the phenomenal growth of the United States by immigration that has made the difference, and even yet the new American-born principle has not gained universal acceptance. This principle, however, played no part in the quarrel over impressment. The American government did not pretend to throw the protecting cloak of American naturalization around the bodies of these British fugitives. The quarrel over impressment turned on the right of search for deserters, and on the abuses which inevitably accompanied the practice.

The right of search was the main point in the dispute, and here the clash between the past and the future stands out clearly. The British position rested on the prerogative of sovereignty to pursue fugitive nationals anywhere up to a line where another sovereignty barred the pursuit. The United States claimed no right to protect American vessels from search in British territorial waters; nor, on the other hand, did Britain claim the right of search within territorial waters of the United States. It was a question of jurisdiction on the high seas, over which there was of course no sovereignty, and there the difference was not over the immunity of government vessels. Though the *Chesapeake* incident has at times led people to suppose the contrary, Britain never asserted the right to search units of the United States Navy. What she did assert, and the United States deny, was the right to search private vessels because this involved no invasion of another sovereignty. Both sides were right, Britain by the old usage, and the United States by a new doctrine then only beginning to take shape: that a country's ships at sea are detached portions of its soil and therefore covered by its sovereignty. Though already admitted for public vessels, it was not yet really established for private ones. Even today this sovereignty is not as complete as that which exists on land or within the limits of territorial waters, and the United States admitted qualification then. The American government recognized, for example, the British right to stop and search private American ships for contraband in time of war.

It was the abuses which accompanied the practice of searching for deserters that inflamed the quarrel, and these abuses occurred on both sides. The British never claimed the right to impress American seamen, but they did impress them as British subjects. It was often impossible to tell the difference between the American and the British members of a crew, for there was no national distinction of language, physical appearance, dress, or manners. British deserters sailing under the Stars and Stripes would insist that they belonged to that flag;

and the officers under whom they were serving, loath to lose valuable hands, would support their contention. A boarding officer in search of men whom he badly needed was judge in his own cause, and there was no real check upon his arbitrary decisions. No officer who seized goods as contraband could touch his share of the prize until it was brought into port and there condemned after a legal trial of the seizure, but there was no such procedure to protect human beings seized on the wide ocean. The only way to rescue an American thus carried off was to prove to the Admiralty that he was an American, and then an order for his release would be issued; but this was a difficult business and painfully slow. . . . As the years passed, the number of kidnaped Americans serving in the Royal Navy mounted until it was several thousand. This right of search and practice of impressment was the British counterpart of the unrestricted submarine campaign conducted by Germany a century later, for it touched American lives, and lives are more precious than goods.

Interference with American trade, the other great issue which the French war raised between the United States and Britain, was a complicated question. . . . The trouble springs from the very nature of war. It is a triangular affair. In addition to the clash of arms between belligerents, it precipitates a clash of interest between belligerent and neutral over intercourse with the enemy. The one would like to stop it completely and the other to continue it without any interruption. Long experience has tended to work out a rough compromise between them, for both have felt the restrain of prudence, the belligerent fearing to push the neutral to the point of open hostility, and the neutral shrinking from resistance that would mean fighting. Hence it came

to be generally recognized that a belligerent could seize and condemn as legal prize any neutral vessel and cargo containing contraband being sent to the enemy country; and also, under the same penalty, could prohibit any neutral vessel, no matter what her cargo, from entering or leaving a blockaded port of the enemy.

All governments admitted that arms and accouterments of war constituted contraband, but there was no common agreement upon the further definition of the term. The textbook writers offered confusing advice. From the conflicting precedents which they recorded, they could deduce only the general principle that other things which might be used by the fighting forces could be treated as contraband when particular circumstances warranted such procedure. A few treaties gave greater precision to the meaning of the word; but there was conflict between them, and each had only a limited application. Thus the original clash of interest survived. Belligerents sought to expand the definition of the term, and neutrals to contract it. Both dressed up selfish interests as legal rights, and the decision between them was left as before to force tempered by prudence. Because the British soon chased the French from the sea, it was the interest of the latter to uphold the narrowest neutral view, and of the former to maintain the opposite, so that over this question the United States became embroiled with Britain and not with France. . . .

More exasperating difficulties grew out of the application of the other principle mentioned above. When was a blockade not a blockade? It was commonly conceded that a blockade had to be officially declared and had to be effective, but there was absolutely no consensus of opinion on what was "effective." Here treaties and classical authorities were of much less assistance than in the definition of contraband. Here Nature intervened to render impossible the formulation of any but a very general rule when it was at last adopted by the principal powers, with the exception of the United States, in the Declaration of Paris in 1856. So variable was the combination of such essential conditions as channels, currents, coasts, and weather, that each application of a blockade was a special problem. . . . As long as the problem of blockade was confined to single ports, it was relatively simple; but, as will be noticed presently, that limitation soon disappeared in the titanic struggle between Britain and the Napoleonic Empire, and it has never returned.

From the ancient and undoubted right of a belligerent to capture private ships and goods of the enemy at sea, sprang other issues between the United States and Britain. One was the principle of "free ships, free goods," which would limit this right by giving immunity to enemy goods, other than contraband, on board neutral vessels. The limitation was so severe that, if enforced, it would have largely destroyed the value of the right, for an enemy could then trade with impunity under the protection of neutral flags. It was a doctrine made by neutrals in the interest of neutrals, to whom it would hand over the carrying trade of belligerents. Its advocates gave it a specious appearance of justice by coupling it with the converse, "enemy ships, enemy goods," which would likewise benefit neutrals by discouraging neutral use of belligerent bottoms. Free ships, free goods, was another of the principles laid down in the Declaration of Paris in 1856. At the time of the French Revolutionary wars, it was a subject of rather violent disagreement. It

was already well on the way to establishment, for it had been written into a number of specific treaties. Even Britain had signed an odd treaty embodying it, but she had never admitted its general application, and she could not do so then without playing into the hands of France. . . . It was the official doctrine of the United States government, but opinion in the country was far from being unanimous in support of it. When Jefferson was Secretary of State, he wrote to Genet: "It cannot be doubted, but that, by the general law of nations, the goods of a friend found in the vessel of an enemy are free, and the goods of an enemy found in the vessel of a friend are lawful prize. . . ."

Of more serious consequence was the disputed right of neutrals in time of war to enter a trade that was shut to them in time of peace. This likewise threatened to destroy the value of the belligerent right to capture enemy property at sea. No compromise principle of any kind had arisen to regulate this issue. It involved two important branches of trade — coasting and colonial. Both were almost universally preserved as strict national monopolies in the period with which we are concerned. If a belligerent, exercising the clear right of capturing enemy ships and cargoes, could drive the enemy from the sea, the enemy would naturally seek relief by temporarily opening its monopoly to neutrals. If they took advantage of this indulgence they would certainly be bringing succor to the distressed enemy. Could neutrals do it and yet remain neutrals?

It was the colonial side of the question which first thrust itself forward, and therefore the first to get any answer. That was in the Seven Years' War, during which the British Empire devoured most of the French Empire overseas. Hard pressed by British maritime superiority, France was unable to supply her West Indies or to bring their produce to Europe under her own flag; and therefore she resorted to the expedient of relaxing her colonial monopoly in favor of neutrals. To counter this novel action, the British prize courts promulgated the novel doctrine which came to be known as "the Rule of the War of 1756," and later simply "the Rule of 1756".... It was naturally a categorical negative to the question just stated. Made in Britain to support the interest of Britain, it was another illustration of law being the declared will of superior force. But there was justice in the contention that a trade prohibited by municipal law during peace should be prohibited by international law during war. It deprived neutrals of no right which they enjoyed prior to the outbreak of war, and it was necessary to preserve the value of an unquestioned belligerent right. It was a new rule called forth by new conditions, and it was promulgated in the only way possible. Yet, however just it might be, it ran counter to the interests of neutrals and of belligerents that suffered from naval impotence; and they would not recognize the validity of this fiat of a single power.

The first American collision with this rule ... nearly precipitated the United States into a declaration of war in the spring of 1794. Indeed Britain had overstepped her own mark by ordering the indiscriminate capture of American vessels trafficking in the French West Indies, for a limited trade in American vessels of small burthen had been legalized before the war; and she drew back just in time. She then contented herself with only a partial application of the rule, ordering the capture of vessels laden in the French West Indies with produce of

those islands and sailing thence for Europe. The fruits of the naval superiority of the belligerent were being shared with a neutral.

The nature of this compromise is worth noting. It was confined to a single neutral, the United States, and it was wholly practical. Britain did not renounce any part of her full right under the Rule of 1756. What she did was done voluntarily, under no pressure from America, for the restrained practice was inaugurated long before people in the United States knew that the unrestrained practice had begun....

The liberality of this compromise, and its adoption by unilateral action, may seem to imply a tacit admission on the part of Britain that the principle she had enunciated to meet new conditions in the Seven Years' War did not apply to the yet newer conditions created by American independence, and therefore should not be applied against the United States. The late Admiral Mahan was inclined to draw this deduction, but it is not quite just. This particular British moderation was simply part and parcel of the regular British policy to keep the interference of belligerent rights with neutral rights down to the minimum necessitated by the exigencies of war. In this instance the interference was considerably less than landlubbers might imagine, for the trade winds blew away much of the hardship imposed on American vessels. They did not have to go very far out of their regular course to call at an American port when sailing from the West Indies to Europe. Yet the situation was fraught with danger.... At any time the British prize courts might shift the basis of their rulings, substituting the "continuous" for the "broken" voyage, and the British government might decide to apply the Rule of 1756 in all its rigor. This decision was never made, but the shift did occur, upsetting the compromise and precipitating trouble.

American action, both public and private, was responsible for destroying the foundation of the British prize-court decisions favorable to the American interest. The doctrine of the broken voyage rested on the assumption that the goods in question were legally imported for use in the United States before they were reëxported. Importation meant the payment of customs duties, and the performance of such operations as unloading, checking, weighing, and storing, all of which involved time and expense. The corresponding operations attendant upon exportation of course added more to the cost. Here were hardships which the trade winds could not blow away, but American ingenuity might remove.

In 1799, Congress passed an act authorizing drawbacks which reduced to a nominal rate the duties paid on certain articles. These, it was observed [by James Stephen, an English critic of America], were "the ordinary and peculiar subjects of trade between Europe and the West-India colonies." This piece of legislation, which would go far to mend what had been broken, remained unnoticed in England for some time, probably because the hostile relations then subsisting between the United States and France blocked its effect upon the operation of the Rule of 1756. But it could not escape attention after the rupture of the Peace of Amiens, when its effect was bound to be felt because Franco-American relations were once more friendly. This effect was enhanced by another mending process which, by contrast, was quite illegal and therefore conducted less openly. There was a constant temptation to cut corners with cargoes in port. Why go through all the motions of importing

and reëxporting, when the same freight was put back in the same hold? Why should Americans suffer this absurd handicap for the benefit of British competitors? Patriotism pulled with profits, private shippers conspired with public officials, and proper papers covered improper performance. Some vessels even cleared with untouched cargoes. What was pious fraud in American ports became plain fraud under British questioning elsewhere. Thus, by congressional enactment and by official connivance, the Rule of 1756 was circumvented in the United States. But it was impossible to mend the broken voyage without ending it. That this was what Americans were doing, the British began to see when the war with France was resumed in the spring of 1803. Almost immediately the modern doctrine of the continuous voyage raised its head in the British prize courts, though it was not until the spring of 1805 that it was finally established by a judgment on appeal [in the famous *Essex* case]. Its establishment doomed American ships and cargoes to capture and condemnation, thereby ruining a lucrative American trade.

Whether neutrals could engage in the coasting trade of an enemy — the other part of the question which had evoked the Rule of 1756 — remained in the background much longer than the problem of colonial trade. . . . Not until some little time after the renewal of hostilities in 1803 did this issue thrust itself forward, and then it was soon obscured by other issues. As Napoleon's power spread on land and Britain's grew on the sea, he was relieved and she was frustrated by neutrals' taking over the coasting trade of his empire. Sooner or later she was bound to strike at their interference in this new sphere as she had struck at their interference in colonial trade during the

Seven Years' War. She held her hand until January, 1807, when, finding a plausible excuse in Napoleon's recent Berlin Decree which was still little more than an empty threat, she outlawed all commerce between ports under his control. Apparently this extension of the Rule of 1756 was directed at northern Europeans, chiefly the Danes, rather than the Americans, but it was plainly recognized that they would feel the blow too. The American government promptly protested that the British action was illegal unless based on "actual blockades," and pointed out that it would ruin a trade which Britain herself recognized as wholly legitimate. The profits of a voyage commonly depended on dropping some cargo here and some there, and on picking up a return cargo in the same way. If an American merchantman had to make the whole exchange in one place, it might as well not go to France at all.

Thus did the issue over the enemy's coasting trade come into the open when the issue over the enemy's colonial trade was finally chased out of its hole by the doctrine of the continuous voyage. Together they were capable of doing great damage to Anglo-American relations, and therefore it is easy to imagine the havoc wrought by the quarrel which soon swallowed them up along with all the other particular issues concerning trade — the quarrel over Napoleon's Berlin and Milan decrees and Britain's equally famous orders-in-council.

To understand these decrees and orders, we should remember that they accompanied the approach of the supreme crisis in the life-and-death struggle between the two powers which were then by far the greatest on earth. Napoleon had come to realize that his position in Europe would never be secure until he subdued Britain, and she that her freedom depended on his downfall. Having had to abandon his projected invasion of the island kingdom because British sea power effectively barred the way, he perforce fell back upon the use of his land power to accomplish by slow strangulation what was impossible by quick assault. Taking advantage of the fact that Britain had stretched her declaration of blockade to cover a considerable length of his northern coast line, he stretched his declaration still farther and justified his action as a proper reprisal. He proclaimed the blockade of the whole of the British Isles.

This was a sort of fantastic and inverted blockade. Napoleon had no navy to enforce it, and his object was not so much to keep goods from reaching Britain as it was to prevent them from leaving. Because of this inversion, however, and also because of the wide extent of his power upon the Continent, he could undertake to enforce the blockade without a navy. This was what he was doing when he ordered the confiscation of all British goods and also, under pain of confiscation, the exclusion of every ship that touched at a British port. By depriving Britain of access to the European market upon which her economic life depended, he calculated that he could soon reduce the nation of traders and manufacturers to cry for mercy. Such, in short, was his Continental System which he began to enforce vigorously in the late summer of 1807. Britain saw that, if he carried it through, she was done. The orders-in-council were her desperate reply. She extended her blockade to every port from which he excluded her ships; and she turned back upon him the provisions of his own decrees, declaring that she would treat as an enemy any ship which, without first going to Britain, sought to enter any port controlled by him.

The position of neutrals became impossible. It would have been much easier for them if they could have chosen to trade either with Britain or with the Napoleonic empire, but this was not the alternative that was forced upon them. The real issue was the Continental System. Would they coöperate with Napoleon in upholding it, or with Britain in undermining it? The question presented a perfect dilemma. A neutral vessel could not approach any European port that was under Napoleon's sway without being liable to seizure, either outside by a ship of the Royal Navy or inside by Napoleon's officials; inside, if it had touched at a British port, or had procured British papers; outside, if it had not. It was a choice between the devil and the deep sea.

Each belligerent was coercing neutrals to serve its own end; and as neutral rights disappeared under the combined pressure, each belligerent defended its departures from the traditional law of nations by accusing the other of prior violations and by blaming neutrals for their nonresistance to these violations. Neutrals, however, could not accept the self-justification of either without shedding their neutrality, nor could they offer resistance to either without running the same risk. Resistance to both was unthinkable. It was then more terribly true than ever that law is what those who can and will enforce it say that it is; and that the principle of reprisal, once let loose, may destroy the other principles of the laws of war. Indeed, the "laws of war" is a contradiction in terms.

Both belligerents this time flouted the United States, and both professed eagerness to resume conformity to traditional law; but each insisted that the other should do it first, or that the Americans should resist with force the coercion of the other. Theoretically, the two belligerents were equally oppressive; but practically, legally, and psychologically they were not. Britain's control of the sea, being greater than Napoleon's control of the land, gave her greater power of enforcement. Much more important was the legal difference. Her seizures were made at sea and therefore, according to her own admission, were a violation of neutral rights under international law, her justification being that it was a necessary reprisal against Napoleon. His seizures, except an occasional capture by a fugitive French frigate or privateer at sea, were all made in port and therefore within the undoubted jurisdiction of his own or a subordinate government. Strictly speaking, his only violation of neutral rights under international law was confined to the occasional captures just mentioned. Napoleon also struck a responsive chord in the United States when he denounced the orders-in-council as designed to establish the economic supremacy of England upon the ruins of the industry and commerce of European countries. Here we approach another fundamental factor in the growing Anglo-American bitterness.

Between Britain and the United States there was a mutual suspicion mounting to a settled conviction that each was using the war to cheat the other out of its rights. The British were exasperated by the paradox of their position. Never had they possessed such complete control of the sea, yet more than ever the seaborne trade of the enemy was escaping from their grasp. As already suggested, neutrals were running off with it and giving it their protection. They were climbing up on the back of the British Navy, whose supremacy persuaded the enemy to hand over this trade; and they were throwing dust in the eyes of British judges, causing them to release as neutral what was really enemy property. By such means not only were they expanding their merchant marine while that of Britain shrank; they were actually robbing her of the profitable prizes of war and also of the crowning prize of a victorious end to the war. In other words, their cupidity had leagued them with the enemy and drawn them into an under-hand war against Britain. The tricks by which they performed the daily miracle of transforming enemy into neutral commerce were publicly exposed, and a new British policy was demanded, by James Stephen in his *War in Disguise, or the Frauds of the Neutral Flags,* a pamphlet of more than two hundred pages which appeared in the fall of 1805. The author knew whereof he spoke, for he was perhaps the leading practitioner in the prize appeal court and he had earlier followed his profession in the West Indies. He probably shared the responsibility for the adoption of the principle of the continuous voyage, but this did not satisfy him. He was positive that there was only one cure for the evil, and that was a rigorous application of the Rule of 1756. Even if it drove neutrals into open hostilities, that would be preferable to this covert war. Britain would then be free to use her strength to strike down those who were injuring her.

Stephen gave forceful expression to a latent but growing feeling of hostility against neutrals in general and Americans in particular. It was directed against Americans in particular because they were gathering by far the greatest harvest at British expense, their mercantile marine having rapidly become the only great rival of Britain's. The pamphlet was very popular, running through three editions in four months. It undoubtedly had a great effect upon public opinion and may even have had some part, as has been supposed, in suggesting the famous orders-in-council. Be this as it may, the chief significance of Stephen's outburst would appear to have been symptomatic rather than causal. The logic of events was teaching Britain that she could not much longer allow neutrals to reap where she had sown.

As British people believed that Americans were abusing their neutral rights to the vital injury of Britain, so were Americans convinced that Britain was abusing her temporary belligerent rights to serve her permanent economic interests and that in doing so she was furtively dealing a dangerous blow at their country. They saw her trying, under cover of the war, to monopolize the commerce of the world. This may seem absurd when we remember that their mercantile marine had enjoyed a phenomenal expansion through the war while hers had suffered a contraction; but we should not overlook some other important considerations. Britain was in a position to do this very thing, international law being what it was and the Royal Navy being virtually supreme upon the sea; and there was no gainsaying the fact that measures which she took to win the war also tended to benefit her own carrying trade and commerce at the expense of others. In the United States this further effect was bound to be regarded as intentional and not just incidental. The adoption of the doctrine of the continuous voyage contained the suggestion that Britain would destroy what she could not appropriate; and the orders-in-council seemed to prove it.

The American reaction appears all the more natural when viewed in the light of the past. Britain had laid herself open to this suspicion by a policy which she, and she alone, had followed for generations. It was the policy of her navigation laws, by which she excluded foreigners from all but a corner of her carrying trade. This application of the monopolistic principle was purposely made to stimulate the growth of the country's merchant marine, and was commonly credited, both at home and abroad, with having made it what it was — the greatest in the world. Another object of the exclusion of foreigners was to deprive them, particularly the Dutch, of their function as middlemen in international trade, and to transfer this function and its profits to England. Not unconsciously had she become the chief storehouse and clearinghouse of the world's commerce, or, to use the language of the day, the great entrepot. She had attained a position where she held the world in fee. It is not surprising, therefore, that non-British eyes saw in the orders-in-council a new and ruthless projection of the old and selfish design. To Americans, of all people, these orders-in-council were particularly offensive. The reason for their peculiar sensitiveness lay in their own history: they were being forced back into the dependence of colonial days. Once more Britain was insisting that they should have no trade of their own, that all their foreign commerce must be under her control. American Independence was at stake! ...

The whole international situation rapidly became much worse in the latter part of 1807 as a consequence of French, British, and American action. The change came before there was any possibility of liquidating the *Chesapeake* affair and quite independently of it, though there can be no doubt that things would not have been so bad if that unfortunate incident had never occurred.

The new turn of events grew out of the mighty struggle in the Old World, which then reached its central climax, and the initial impetus came from France.

Napoleon's smashing victory over Russia at Friedland led him to believe that he had completed his mastery over Europe and could therefore make his Continental System work the destruction of England's power. Having persuaded Alexander to apply it in Russia, he proceeded to enforce his Berlin Decree vigorously in the rest of the Continent. His orders were issued in August, and by the end of the month the news of wholesale seizures startled London. There it became practically impossible to get insurance for shipments to the Continent, so that they ceased for the time being. Ostensibly in retaliation for the way Britain then struck back at him, Napoleon tightened his system on December 17, 1807, when he issued the Milan Decree. This announced that any neutral ship, together with its cargo, sailing from a British port or having submitted to British search had lost its neutral character and become lawful prize.

The British action which thus stirred his ire was the issuance of the famous orders-in-council of November 11, 1807, modified and developed by subsequent orders, declaring a blockade of all countries in Napoleon's system, together with their colonies, and condemning their produce as lawful prize. This was precisely the weapon he had aimed at Britain in his Berlin Decree. She claimed that she had a right to do to him what he would do to her; and at the same time she prided herself on being more considerate of neutrals, for she made a number of important exceptions in further provisions to be noticed presently.

Such assertions were delusive. There were fundamental differences between the two belligerents and what they were trying to do to each other. Napoleon would have stopped all trade from anywhere with Britain, but he could not; whereas she could have prevented all intercourse with the French Empire and its dependencies, but she would not. He could not, because he had no navy and she possessed a mighty one; she would not, because she felt that her life and liberty depended on continued access to the European market, from which he would exclude her utterly by means of his land power. In one respect their sweeping declarations of blockade were alike. Both were dishonest, being designed to cover only a partial though effective execution. Her object, however, was the opposite of his. Hence her tenderness toward neutrals.

Britain announced that neutral vessels might pass with impunity through the blockade of Europe if they were cleared from, or bound for, a British port in the Old World. They would serve her pur-pose. The strong continental demand for her wares would see to that; and she revised her navigation and customs laws to legalize the introduction of return cargoes comprising goods of enemy origin for domestic consumption or re-export. Another "concession" to neutrals was that of direct trade with enemy colonies; for the British fleet effectively isolated them from Napoleon's dangerous system, and the British government was anxious to avoid unnecessary pressure upon neutrals lest she lose their indispensable aid in European waters. Even the produce of enemy colonies might thus find its way to their mother country, Britain collecting equalizing duties to protect the produce of her own colonies. No concession, however, was to protect ships complying with a new regulation of Napoleon, by which his agents abroad certified that their cargoes contained nothing of British origin. Such ships and cargoes were to be confiscated.

HENRY ADAMS, the great grandson of John and the grandson of John Quincy, left a teaching position at Harvard to write a history of his country during the administrations of Jefferson and Madison. This work, perhaps the greatest single accomplishment of an American historian, appeared in nine volumes between 1889 and 1891. In vigorous prose, as the selections below show, Adams castigates British policy towards the United States and suggests the depth of the challenge it presented American honor and interests.*

▶

The Chesapeake and the Orders in Council of November 1807

That the accident which then happened should not have happened long before was matter for wonder, considering the arbitrary character of British naval officers and their small regard for neutral rights. For many years the open encouragement offered to the desertion of British seamen in American ports had caused extreme annoyance to the royal navy; and nowhere had this trouble been more serious than at Norfolk. Early in 1807 a British squadron happened to be lying within the Capes watching for some French frigates which had taken refuge at Annapolis. One or more of these British ships lay occasionally in Hampton Roads, or came to the navy-yard at Gos-

port for necessary repairs. Desertions were of course numerous; even the American ships-of-war had much difficulty from loss of men, — and March 7 a whole boat's crew of the British sixteen-gun sloop "Halifax" made off with the jolly-boat and escaped to Norfolk. The commander of the "Halifax" was informed that these men had enlisted in the American frigate "Chesapeake," then under orders for the Mediterranean. He complained to the British consul and to Captain Decatur, but could get no redress. He met two of the deserters in the streets of Norfolk, and asked them why they did not return. One of them, Jenkin Ratford by name, replied, with abuse

*Henry Adams, *History of the United States During the Second Administration of Thomas Jefferson,* Charles Scribner's Sons, New York, 1890, vol. II, pp. 1-3, 9-16, 18-20, 81-83, 92-93, 97-104.

and oaths, that he was in the land of liberty and would do as he liked. The British minister at Washington also made complaint that the three deserters from the "Melampus" frigate had enlisted on the "Chesapeake." The Secretary of the Navy ordered an inquiry, which proved that the three men in question, one of whom was a negro, were in fact on board the "Chesapeake," but that they were native Americans who had been improperly impressed by the "Melampus," and therefore were not subjects for reclamation by the British government. The nationality was admitted, and so far as these men were concerned the answer was final; but the presence of Jenkin Ratford, an Englishman, on board the "Chesapeake" under the name of Wilson escaped notice.

The admiral in command of the British ships on the North American station was George Cranfield Berkeley, a brother of the Earl of Berkeley. To him, at Halifax, the British officers in Chesapeake Bay reported their grievances; and Admiral Berkeley, without waiting for authority from England, issued the following orders, addressed to all the ships under his command: —

"Whereas many seamen, subjects of his Britannic Majesty, and serving in his ships and vessels as per margin ["Bellona," "Belleisle," "Triumph," "Chichester," "Halifax," "Zenobia"], while at anchor in the Chesapeake, deserted and entered on board the United States frigate called the 'Chesapeake,' and openly paraded the street of Norfolk, in sight of their officers, under the American flag, protected by the magistrates of the town and the recruiting officer belonging to the above-mentioned American frigate, which magistrates and naval officer refused giving them up, although demanded by his Britannic Majesty's consul, as well as the captains of the ships from which the said men had deserted:

"The captains and commanders of his Majesty's ships and vessels under my command are therefore hereby required and directed, in case of meeting with American frigate 'Chesapeake' at sea, and without the limits of the United States, to show to the captain of her this order, and to require to search his ship for deserters from the before-mentioned ships, and to proceed and search for the same; and if a similar demand should be made by the American, he is to be permitted to search for any deserters from their service, according to the customs and usage of civilized nations on terms of peace and amity with each other...."

The order, dated June 1, 1807, was sent to Chesapeake Bay by the frigate "Leopard," commanded by Captain S. P. Humphreys.... The "Leopard" arrived at Lynnhaven on the morning of June 21; and Captain Humphreys reported his arrival and orders to Captain John Erskine Douglas of the "Bellona," a line-of-battle ship, then lying with "Melampus" frigate in Lynnhaven Bay, enjoying the hospitality of the American government.... The next morning, June 22, at 4 A.M., the "Leopard" made sail, and two hours later re-anchored a few miles to the eastward, and about three miles north of Cape Henry Lighthouse....

At a quarter-past seven o'clock on the morning of June 22 the "Chesapeake" got under way [in Hampton Roads] with a fair breeze.... At nine o'clock, passing Lynnhaven Bay, the officers on deck noticed the "Bellona" and "Melampus" at anchor. The "Leopard" lay farther out, and the "Bellona" was observed to be signalling.... Had Barron been able to read the "Bellona's" signals he would have suspected nothing, for they contained merely an order to the "Leopard" to weigh and reconnoitre in the southeast by east. The British squadron was in the habit of keeping a cruiser outside to overhaul merchant-vessels; and when the "Leopard" stood out to sea, the officers of the "Chesapeake" naturally supposed that this was her errand. . . .

At about half-past three o'clock, both ships being eight or ten miles southeast by east of Cape Henry, the "Leopard" came down before the wind, and rounding to, about half a cable's length to windward, hailed, and said she had despatches for the commodore. Barron returned the hail and replied, "We will heave to and you can send your boat on board of us. . . ."

Barron went to his cabin to receive the British officer, whose boat came alongside. At a quarter before four o'clock Lieutenant Meade from the "Leopard" arrived on board, and was shown by Captain Gordon to the commodore's cabin. He delivered the following note:—

"The captain of his Britannic Majesty's ship 'Leopard' has the honor to enclose the captain of the United States ship 'Chesapeake' an order from the Honorable Vice-Admiral Berkeley, commander-in-chief of his Majesty's ships on the North American station, respecting some deserters from the ships (therein mentioned) under his command, and supposed to be now serving as part of the crew of the 'Chesapeake.'

"The captain of the 'Leopard' will not presume to say anything in addition to what the commander-in-chief has stated, more than to express a hope that every circumstance respecting them may be adjusted in a manner that the harmony subsisting between the two countries may remain undisturbed."

Having read Captain Humphrey's note, Commodore Barron took up the enclosed order signed by Admiral Berkeley. This order, as the note mentioned, designated deserters from certain ships. Barron knew that he had on board three deserters from the "Melampus," and that these three men had been the only deserters officially and regularly demanded by the British minister. His first thought

was to look for the "Melampus" in the admiral's list; and on seeing that Berkeley had omitted it, Barron inferred that his own assurance would satisfy Captain Humphreys, and that the demand of search, being meant as a mere formality, would not be pressed. He explained to the British lieutenant the circumstances relating to the three men from the "Melampus," and after some consultation with Dr. Bullus, who was going out as consul to the Mediterranean, he wrote to Captain Humphreys the following reply: —

"I know of no such men as you describe. The officers that were on the recruiting service for this ship were particularly instructed by the Government, through me, not to enter any deserters from his Britannic Majesty's ships, nor do I know of any being here. I am also instructed never to permit the crew of any ship that I command to be mustered by any other but their own officers. It is my disposition to preserve harmony, and I hope this answer to your despatch will prove satisfactory. . . ."

Meanwhile, at a quarter-past four the officer of the deck sent down word that the British frigate had a signal flying. The lieutenant understood it for a signal of recall, as he had been half an hour away, and as soon as the letter could be written he hurried with it to his boat. No sooner had he left the cabin than Barron sent for Gordon and showed him the letters which had passed. Although the commodore hoped that the matter was disposed of, and assumed that Captain Humphreys would give some notice in case of further action, he could not but feel a show of energy to be proper, and he directed Gordon to order the gun-deck to be cleared. Instantly the officers began to prepare the ship for action. . . .

That Captain Humphreys felt it necessary to gain and retain every possible advantage was evident from his conduct. He could not afford to run the risk of defeat in such an undertaking; and knowing that the "Chesapeake" needed time to prepare for battle, he felt not strong enough to disregard her power of resistance, as he might have done had he commanded a ship of the line. To carry out his orders with as little loss as possible was his duty; for the consequences, not he but his admiral was to blame. Without a moment of delay, edging nearer, he hailed and cried: "Commodore Barron, you must be aware of the necessity I am under of complying with the order of my commander-in-chief."

Hardly more than five minutes passed between the moment when the British officer left Commodore Barron's cabin and the time when Barron was hailed. To get the ship ready for action required fully half an hour.... Barron, aware that his only chance was to gain time, remained at the gangway and replied through his trumpet: "I do not hear what you say." Captain Humphreys repeated his hail, and Barron again replied that he did not understand. The "Leopard" immediately fired a shot across the "Chesapeake's" bow; a minute later another shot followed; and in two minutes more, at half-past four o'clock, the "Leopard" poured her whole broadside of solid shot and canister, at the distance of one hundred and fifty or two hundred feet, point-blank into the helpless American frigate....

The British account, which was very exact, said that the "Leopard's" fire lasted fifteen minutes,— from 4:30 to 4:45 P.M.,— during which time three full broadsides were discharged without return. No one could demand that Commodore Barron should subject his crew and ship to a longer trial when he had no hope of success.... The official survey,

taken the next day, showed twenty-two round-shot in the "Chesapeake's" hull, ten shot-holes in the sails, all three masts badly injured, the rigging much cut by grape, three men killed, eight severely and ten slight wounded, including Commodore Barron — which proved that of the seventy or eighty discharges from the "Leopard's" guns a large proportion took effect.

After enduring this massacre for fifteen minutes, while trying to fire back at least one gun for the honor of the ship, Commodore Barron ordered the flag to be struck. It was hauled down; and as it touched the taffrail one gun was discharged from the gun-deck sending a shot into the "Leopard." This single gun was fired by the third lieutenant, Allen, by means of a live coal which he brought in his fingers from the galley.

The boats of the "Leopard" then came on board, bringing several British officers, who mustered the ship's company. They selected the three Americans who had deserted from the "Melampus," and were therefore not included in Berkeley's order. Twelve or fifteen others were pointed out as English deserters, but these men were not taken. After a search of the ship, Jenkin Ratford was dragged out of the coal-hole; and this discovery alone saved Captain Humphreys from the blame of committing an outrage not only lawless but purposeless. At about seven o'clock the British officer left the ship, taking with them the three Americans and Jenkin Ratford. Immediately afterward Commodore Barron sent Lieutenant Allen on board the "Leopard" with a brief letter to Captain Humphreys: —

"I consider the frigate 'Chesapeake' your prize, and am ready to deliver her to any officer authorized to receive her. By the return of the boat I shall expect your answer."

The British captain immediately replied as follows:

"Having to the utmost of my power fulfilled the instructions of my commander-in-chief, I have nothing more to desire, and must in consequence proceed to join the remainder of the squadron,— repeating that I am ready to give you every assistance in my power, and do most sincerely deplore that any lives should have been lost in the execution of a service which might have been adjusted more amicably, not only with respect to ourselves but the nations to which we respectively belong."

At eight o'clock Barron called a council of officers to consider what was best to be done with the ship, and it was unanimously decided to return to the Roads and wait orders. Disgraced, degraded, with officers and crew smarting under a humiliation that was never forgotten or forgiven, the unlucky "Chesapeake" dragged her way back to Norfolk. . . .

[The attack upon the *Chesapeake* virtually monopolized America's attention for some months. Private vessels on the high seas were scarcely molested until the late summer of 1807.]

Napoleon's Berlin Decree of Nov. 21, 1806, had remained till then almost a dead letter. The underwriters at Lloyds, alarmed at first by the seizures made under that decree, recovered courage between April and August, 1807, so far as to insure at low rates neutral vessels bound to Holland and Hamburg. This commerce attracted Napoleon's notice. August 19 he threatened his brother Louis, King of Holland, to send thirty thousand troops into his kingdom if the ports were not shut; August 24 he sent positive orders that his decree of Berlin should be executed in Holland; and in the last days of August news reached London that a general seizure of neutral vessels had taken place at Amsterdam. From that moment no ship could obtain insurance, and trade with the Continent ceased. Soon afterward the American ship "Horizon" was condemned by the French courts under the Berlin Decree, and no one could longer doubt that the favor hitherto extended to American commerce had also ceased.

These dates were important, because upon them hung the popular defence of Perceval's subsequent Orders in Council. No argument in favor of these orders carried so much weight in England as the assertion that America had acquiesced in Napoleon's Berlin Decree. The President had in fact submitted to the announcement of Napoleon's blockade, as he had submitted to Sir William Scott's decisions, Lord Howick's Order in Council, the blockade of New York, and the custom of impressment, without effectual protest; but the Berlin Decree was not enforced against American commerce until about Sept. 1, 1807, and no one in America knew of the enforcement, or could have acted upon it, before the British government took the law into its own hands.

The month of September passed, and the British ministry was sufficiently busy with the bombardment of Copenhagen and the assault on the "Chesapeake," without touching neutral trade; but October 1 Lord Castlereagh wrote a letter to Perceval, urging retaliation upon France in order to make her feel that Napoleon's anti-commercial system was useless, and in order to assert for future guidance the general principle that England would reject any peace which did not bring commerce with it. The idea presented by Castlereagh was clear and straightforward,— the double-or-quits of a gambler; and however open to the charge of ignorance or violence, it was not mean or dishonest. . . .

By the end of October all the Cabinet opinions were in Perceval's hand's, and he began the task of drafting the proposed orders. His original draft contained an elaborate preamble, asserting that Napoleon's decrees violated the laws of nations, which Perceval broadly maintained were binding on one belligerent only when the obligation was reciprocally acknowledged by the order; that neutrals had not resented and resisted the outrage, "nor interposed with effect for obtaining the revocation of those orders, but on the contrary the same have been recently reinforced;" that Lord Howick's retaliatory order had served only to encourage Napoleon's attempts; that his Majesty had a right to declare all the dominions of France and her allies in a state of blockade; but "not forgetting the interests of neutral nations, and still desirous of retaliating upon the commerce of his enemies with as little prejudice to those interests" as was consistent with his purpose, he would for the present prohibit only trade which neutrals might be disposed to pursue in submission to the French decrees, and require that such trade should pass to or from some British port.

Then followed the order, which prohibited all neutral trade with the whole European sea-coast from Copenhagen to Trieste, leaving only the Baltic open. No American vessel should be allowed to enter any port in Europe from which British vessels were excluded, unless the American should clear from some British port under regulations to be prescribed at a future time. . . .

As the Cabinet came closer to the point, the political, or retaliatory, object of the new order disappeared, and its commercial character was exclusively set forth. In a letter written about November 30, by Spencer Perceval to Charles Abbot, Speaker of the House of Commons, not a word was said of retaliation, or of any political motive in this process of "recasting the law of trade and navigation, as far as belligerent principles are concerned, for the whole world."

"The short principle is," said Perceval, "that trade in British produce and manufactures, and trade either from a British port or with a British destination, is to be protected as much as possible. For this purpose all the countries where French influence prevails to exclude the British flag shall have no trade but to or from this country, or from its allies. All other countries, the few that remain strictly neutral (with the exception of the colonial trade, which backward and forward direct they may carry on), cannot trade but through this being done as an ally with any of the countries connected with France. If therefore we can accomplish our purpose, it will come to this,— that either those countries will have no trade, or they must be content to accept it through us. This is a formidable and tremendous state of the world; but all the part of it which is particularly harassing to English interests was existing through the new severity with which Bonaparte's decrees of exclusion against our trade were called into action. Our proceeding does not aggravate our distress from it. If he can keep out our trade he will; and he would do so if he could, independent of our orders. Our orders only add this circumstance: *they say to the enemy, 'If you will have none; and as to so much of any trade as you can carry on yourselves, or others carry on with you through us, if you admit it you shall pay for it.*[1] The only trade, cheap and untaxed, which you shall have shall be either direct from us, in our own produce and manufactures, or from our allies, whose increased prosperity will be an advantage to us.' "

These private expressions implied that retaliation upon France for her offence

[1] Italics supplied — Ed.

against international law was a pretence on the part of Perceval and Canning, under the cover of which they intended to force British commerce upon France contrary to French wishes. The act of Napoleon in excluding British produce from French dominions violated no rule of international law, and warranted no retaliation except an exclusion of French produce from British dominions. The rejoinder, "If you will not have *our* trade you shall have *none*," was not good law, if law could be disputed when affirmed by men like Lord Eldon and Lord Stowell, echoed by courts, parliaments, and press,— not only in private, but in public; not only in 1807, but for long years afterward; and not only at moments, but without interruption.

Thus Canning, although he warned Perceval against betraying the commercial object of his orders, instructed Erskine at Washington to point out that American ships might still bring colonial produce to England, under certain regulations, for re-export to France. "The object of these regulations will be the establishment of such a protecting duty as shall prevent the enemy from obtaining the produce of his own colonies at a cheaper rate than that of the colonies of Great Britain." Not to distress France, but to encourage British trade, was, according to Canning, the object of this "political" weapon.

Thus Perceval, in the debate of Feb. 5, 1808, in discussing the policy of his order, affirmed that the British navy had been "rendered useless by neutral ships carrying to France all that it was important for France to obtain." The rule of 1756, he said, would not have counteracted this result,— a much stronger measure was necessary; and it was sound policy "to endeavor to force a market." Lord Bathurst, a few days afterward,

very frankly told the House that "the object of these orders was to regulate that which could not be prohibited,— the circuitous trade through this country,"— in order that the produce of enemies' colonies might "be subjected to a duty sufficiently high to prevent its having the advantage over our own colonial produce;" and Lord Hawkesbury, in the same debate, complained that neutrals supplied colonial produce to France at a much less rate than the English paid for it. "To prevent this," he said, "was the great object of the Orders in Council." James Stephen's frequent arguments in favor of the orders turned upon the commercial value of the policy as against neutrals; while George Rose, Vice-President of the Board of Trade, went still further, and not only avowed, in the face of Parliament, the hope that these Orders in Council would make England the emporium of all trade in the world, but even asserted, in an unguarded moment of candor, that it was a mistake to call the orders retaliatory,— they were a system of self-defence, a plan to protect British commerce.

Thus, too, the orders themselves, while licensing the export through England to France of all other American produce, imposed a prohibitive duty on the export of cotton, on the ground — as Canning officially informed the American government — that France had pushed her cotton manufactures to such an extent as to make it expedient for England to embarrass them.

According to the public and private avowals of all the Ministry, the true object of Perceval's orders was, not to force a withdrawal of the Berlin Decree so far as it violated international law, but to protect British trade from competition. Perceval did not wish to famish France, but to feed her. His object was commercial, not political; his policy aimed at checking the commerce of America in order to stimulate the commerce of England. The pretence that this measure had retaliation for its object and the vindication of international law for its end was a legal fiction, made to meet the objections of America and to help Canning in maintaining a position which he knew to be weak.

After this long discussion, and after conferences not only with his colleagues in the Cabinet, but also with George Rose, Vice-President of the Board of Trade, with James Stephen, who was in truth the author of the war on neutrals, and with a body of merchants from the city,— at last, Nov. 11, 1807, Spencer Perceval succeeded in getting his General Order approved in Council. In its final shape this famous document differed greatly from the original draft. In deference to Lord Bathurst's objections, the sweeping doctrine of retaliation was omitted, so that hardly an allusion to it was left in the text; the assertion that neutrals had acquiesced in the Berlin Decree was struck out; the preamble was reduced, by Lord Eldon's advice, to a mere mention of the French pretended blackade, and of Napoleon's real prohibition of British commerce, followed by a few short paragraphs reciting that Lord Howick's order of Jan. 7, 1807, had "not answered the desired purpose either of compelling the enemy to recall those orders or of inducing neutral nations to interpose with effect to obtain their revocation, but on the contrary the same have been recently enforced with increased rigor;" and then, with the blunt assertion that "his Majesty, under these circumstances, finds himself compelled to take further measures for asserting and vindicating his just rights," Perceval,

without more apology, ordered in effect that all American commerce, except that to Sweden and the West Indies, should pass through some British port and take out a British license.

The exceptions, the qualifications, and the verbiage of the British Orders need no notice. The ablest British merchants gave up in despair the attempt to understand them; and as one order followed rapidly upon another, explaining, correcting, and developing Perceval's not too lucid style, the angry Liberals declared their belief that he intended no man to understand them without paying two guineas for a legal opinion, with the benefit of a chance to get a directly contrary opinion for the sum of two guineas more. Besides the express provisions contained in the Order of November 11, it was understood that American commerce with the enemies of England must not only pass through British ports with British license, but that colonial produce would be made to pay a tax to the British Treasury to enhance its price, while cotton would not be allowed to enter France.

The general intention, however confused, was simple. After November 11, 1807, any American vessel carrying any cargo was liable to capture if it sailed for any port in Europe from which the British flag was excluded. In other words, American commerce was made English.

This measure completed, diplomacy was to resume its work. Even Canning's audacity might be staggered to explain how the government of the United States could evade war after it should fairly understand the impressment Proclamation of October 17, the Order in Council of November 11, and the Instructions of George Henry Rose,— who was selected by Canning as his special envoy for the adjustment of the "Leopard's" attack on the "Chesapeake," and who carried orders which made adjustment impossible. Such outrages could be perpetrated only upon a helpless people. Even in England, where Jefferson's pacific policy was well understood, few men believed that peace could be longer preserved.

Jefferson, a man of peace, refused to be propelled toward war by the *Chesapeake* affair or by rumors of the forthcoming orders in council. Instead, he suggested that American ships and goods be withdrawn from the seas. In the next selection, LEONARD D. WHITE, the author of four impressive volumes weighing the administrative success of American Presidents, describes the machinery of the embargo and the ultimate defeat of Jefferson's policy.*

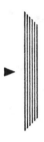

The Embargo

Three days before Christmas 1807, Congress adopted Thomas Jefferson's recommendation to impose an embargo upon all American vessels sailing for foreign ports. After only four days' debate, behind closed doors, the Republican majority thus committed the executive branch to a greater test of its moral authority and administrative capacity than it had yet endured. A President, bound by theory and personal preference to the restriction and dispersion of power, was driven by events to an extraordinary expansion and concentration of power. Receptive in his youth to a revolution every twenty years, he had to yield before one growing under his own hand. Opposed to the use of force against citizens reluctant to pay the excise tax on

whiskey in 1794, he marshaled force of every available sort in 1808 against citizens reluctant to forego what they considered their right to sail the high seas.

Jefferson conceived the embargo as an alternative, indeed the only available alternative, to war. It was an attempt at peaceable coercion of the greatest naval power and the greatest land power of his generation. It could be defended not merely by what might have been thought the intrinsic merit of peaceable coercion, but also by the utter impossibility in the late autumn of 1807 of deciding whether to declare war against the greatest naval power, or the greatest land power, or both; for each was equally guilty of assault on American rights and interests. Although the President thought of the

*From *The Jeffersonians: a Study in Administrative History, 1801-1829*, by Leonard D. White, pp. 423-427, 431-432, 451, 460-461, 468-472. Copyright 1951 by The Macmillan Company, and used with their permission.

embargo as an attempt to coerce these two great European powers by commercial pressure, in fact the embargo drove his Administration into an attempt to coerce a large, powerful, active, and hostile part of his fellow citizens. To this intermediate end, essential for the attainment of his greater purposes, Jefferson asked for power and more power; and upon the use of the authority which his Republican friends yielded, he became more and more insistent, asking commerce, agriculture, and industry to be as nothing before the great object he set himself.

In the end he was defeated in his major purpose of securing concessions from England or France; and in the application of force to his fellow citizens he drove resistance almost to the point of rebellion in New England and upper New York. The effort was a tragic one, the tragedy enhanced by the greatness of the goal that might have been attained. Jefferson was broken spiritually by his failure. He became, as he said himself, a mere spectator of events after December 1808, and finally was obliged to sign the bill abandoning the great experiment three days before he left public life forever.

The Embargo Acts

Jefferson's brief message of December 18, 1807, merely suggested that Congress would "doubtless perceive all the advantages which may be expected from an inhibition of the departure of our vessels from the ports of the United States." His intention was "to keep our seamen and property from capture, and to starve the offending nations." He hoped to gain time, to call commerce home to safety, "to put the towns and harbors ... into a condition of defence," and to prepare for the restoration of the freedom of the seas.

The wisdom and efficiency of the means to the end were not so apparent to Jefferson's advisers as they were to the President himself, whose naturally sanguine temperament discounted any serious problem of enforcement. Gallatin, who had to carry the main burden, told Jefferson plainly that he had no confidence in the enterprise. He notified the President:

... In every point of view, privations, sufferings, revenue, effect on the enemy, politics at home, &c., I prefer war to a permanent embargo.

Governmental prohibitions do always more mischief than had been calculated; and it is not without much hesitation that a statesman should hazard to regulate the concerns of individuals as if he could do it better than themselves.

... As to the hope that it may ... induce England to treat us better, I think it entirely groundless.

Robert Smith, Secretary of the Navy, opposed the embargo, calling it "this mischief-making busybody." No evidence of Madison's private views on the embargo has come to hand nor is there any indication that he took part in working out enforcement policy or in applying enforcement measures. His correspondent, Morgan Lewis, warned him that the influence of the embargo on domestic affairs "will be unpleasant," and that a section of the Republicans were using the embargo as a means of putting George Clinton in the White House — disquieting news to an heir apparent. Monroe, not then in the government but watching events closely from near-by Virginia, referred to "many impolitick measures," the context suggesting the embargo and its successor policies. He declared that "the embargo supported a

very dangerous conflict at home, hazarding the republican cause, union, &c. ...."
Vice President George Clinton was reported in January 1809 as "most outrageous against the Embargo. Says 'tis damning the principle of Republicanism." Governor Sullivan of Massachusetts, a staunch Republican, warned Jefferson of the danger to internal peace in case of conflict with England. But as between war and the experiment of peaceable coercion, Jefferson did not waver. ". . . it was better," he said, "to take the chance of one year by the embargo, within which the orders & decrees producing it may be repealed, or peace take place in Europe, which may secure peace to us. . . ."

The embargo act of December 22, 1807, was directed only against American vessels in the foreign trade known as *registered*, or *sea-letter, vessels*. It was assumed that they might be employed temporarily in the coastwise trade; but to discourage any of them from touching at a foreign port while at sea, the master, owner, consignee, or factor was required to give bond in a sum double the value of the vessel and cargo to land the goods in some port of the United States, "dangers of the sea excepted." Foreign vessels lying in port were allowed to depart, with such cargo as they might have had on board. . . .

[The first Embargo Act proving inadequate, various supplements were passed in the session of 1807-1808.] The mandate of Congress to citizens was simple and straightforward: the movement of American ships in foreign commerce was to stop; exports of specie and goods by land or sea were to cease. To enforce this mandate a number of administrative weapons were made available.

1. Formal clearance of all coastwise vessels, large or small, with heavy bond on coast-

wise, fishing, and whaling vessels not to touch at foreign ports.
2. Prohibition of coastwise trade to American ports adjacent to foreign territory, except individual voyages specifically authorized by the President; exclusion of foreign vessels from the coastwise trade.
3. Lading of vessels only under the immediate inspection of a revenue officer.
4. Authority vested in commanders of revenue cutters and naval vessels to stop a vessel on suspicion, even on the high seas.
5. Authority vested in collectors to detain a vessel on suspicion; release could be granted only by specific direction of the President.
6. Authority vested in collectors to take into custody unusual deposits of goods adjacent to foreign territory.

To the mandate of Congress bidding all foreign voyages to cease there were two exceptions. These exceptions, placed in personal custody of Thomas Jefferson, were:

1. To proceed to a foreign port under the act of December 22, 1807. . . . Jefferson allowed no private vessel this permission.
2. To send a vessel in ballast to a foreign port to bring back property of American citizens held before December 22, 1807. . . .

Resistance to the embargo was . . . substantial and violations were frequent. The spectacular success of adventurous violators, however, ought not to conceal the fact that the embargo came much closer to success than failure so far as the immediate object of keeping American ships in harbor and American goods out of foreign hands was concerned. Despite all the trouble on the New England coast and elsewhere, despite defiance on the Canadian border, the agents of the federal government made a remarkable record in shutting off foreign commerce by sea and by land. In the spring and summer of 1808 goods and merchandise were smuggled out in considerable quantities, but even at the height of this illegal exportation, the bulk of American shipping lay idle in port, under the effective control of the government....

...Every power granted by Congress was put in motion — the punitive bonds and penalties, the restraint of vessels in the coastwise trade, the prohibition of all exports to foreign places, the detention of ships, the seizure of unusual deposits, the deployment of the navy, the assignment of militia, and the use of the regulars. Seizures and forfeitures multiplied despite the indisposition of New England juries to convict and the hostile intervention of the state courts, despite the harassing suits against collectors and occasional outbreaks of violence.... [Ultimately, after passage of the Enforcement Act of 1809,] the President had powers so vast that in fact no vessel could sail if he specified that it should swing at anchor. All that was left was for Congress to authorize the collectors to seize the rudders and put them under lock and key. Of this act, Henry Adams wrote, "It was a terrible measure, and in comparison with its sweeping grants of arbitrary power, all previous enactments of the United States Congress sank into comparative insignificance." It was the death blow to the embargo.

The embargo was a terminable policy, an experiment which had to have a conclusion, successful or otherwise, within a brief period of time. Jefferson acknowledged in the early summer of 1808, writing to Thomas Leib: "It is true, the time will come when we must abandon it. But if this is before the repeal of the orders of council, we must abandon it only for a state of war. The day is not distant, when that will be preferable to a longer continuance of the embargo." By midsummer Robert Smith, Secretary

of the Navy, privately told Gallatin that the embargo should be abandoned. "Most fervently ought we to pray," he wrote, "to be relieved from the various embarrassments of this said embargo." By the end of the year Gallatin himself prophesied that the Republican majority would not adhere to the embargo much longer.

However, in his eighth annual message, November 8, 1808, Jefferson gave no sign of bringing it to end. He recognized that the suspension of foreign commerce was a subject of concern, but praised the consequent growth of manufacturers. On the problem of enforcement he noted that some "small and special detachments" of militia had been required, but asserted that, "By the aid of these and of the armed vessels called into service in other quarters the spirit of disobedience and abuse, which manifested itself early and with sensible effect while we were unprepared to meet it, has been considerably repressed." The initial response of Congress was not to move toward repeal, but toward more rigorous enforcement.

The storm was nevertheless gathering strength and in a sudden burst late in the session swept all before it. On November 25, 1808, there had been read in the Senate the Resolutions of the Massachusetts General Court, speaking ominously of the extreme and increasing pressure upon the people and of the danger to "our domestic peace, and the union of these States." The resolutions instructed the Massachusetts Senators, and requested the Representatives, to use their "most strenuous exertions" to secure repeal.... Sentiment in most of New England was hardening, ... and the drastic terms of the enforcement act of January 9, 1809, made opposition more bitter. Disunion was feared by statesmen such as John Quincy Adams and Joseph B. Varnum, Speaker of the House, and Jefferson himself recorded that Congress fell under the belief that the alternative was civil war or repeal.

The patience of the merchants also was giving out. Ships had been loaded in the fall of 1808 in the expectation that the embargo would be terminated when Congress met in December. Instead Congress put on the books "the ferocious amending act" of January 9, 1809, which forced owners either to unload their cargoes or give heavy bonds. "This," said Heaton, "was the last straw."[1] By the end of March 1809 there were forty ships, embargo breakers, in Liverpool, and more expected. Rumors were circulating in January 1809 that undermined whatever moral authority the embargo then possessed: "Have just got accounts tis coming off very fast Eastward." Gallatin had already sensed the advancing crisis and in November 1808 had exhorted his forces. "I rely at this critical moment," he wrote the collectors, "equally on your vigilance in carrying that object [i.e., enforcement of the embargo] into effect, and on your discretion in doing it in such a manner as will give no grounds of complaint to any but those who intend to disregard the law."

Spring optimism thus faded into summer despair, autumn determination was followed by winter crisis. On March 1, 1809, Jefferson signed a bill repealing the embargo and substituting nonintercourse with England, France, and their possessions. His great experiment collapsed, as he said, "in a kind of panic" among his own party members in Congress. Within three days he left public office. At the close of his life, he recorded:

"I saw the necessity of abandoning it [the embargo], and instead of effecting our purpose by this peaceful weapon, we must fight it out, or break the Union."

Jefferson believed, nevertheless, that peaceable coercion in the form of the embargo would have succeeded, given time and determination. He realized, as he wrote William Short when he was packing for Monticello, "Our embargo has worked hard." But as conflict with Britain came to an end in 1815, he declared that "a continuance of the embargo for two months longer would have prevented our war...." He believed the margin was always narrow between an accommodation induced by want in England and war, and he clung to the prospect of peace....

Success or failure has to be measured by two different considerations: was the embargo successful in stopping American exports; was it successful in bringing either England or France to terms, the real objective? Measured by the latter criterion, the embargo was not a success. Neither France nor England was seriously embarrassed by the lack of American flour, provisions, and other goods. Jennings concluded on this aspect of the matter, "The embargo as an economic means of forcing the European nations to rescind their obnoxious orders and decrees was consequently a failure."[2]

The embargo was more nearly successful from the point of view of stopping the movement of American ships and goods to foreign ports, although even here administrative means were not wholly adequate to the immediate end. The major administrative question was whether the government possessed a system strong enough, reliable enough, and

[1] Herbert Heaton, "Non-Importation, 1806-1812," *Journal of Economic History,* vol. I, no. 2 (November 1941), p. 191.

[2] Walter W. Jennings, *The American Embargo, 1807-1809,* Iowa City, 1921, p. 93.

equipped with the necessary legal authority and physical power to enforce the embargo. The record showed that such a system existed, had been given adequate powers by the emergency legislation, and had discovered within itself the moral authority and determination to reach a substantial degree of success.

HERBERT HEATON, an Englishman by birth but long a professor at the University of Minnesota, is a leading economic historian. In addition to providing a convenient summary of the various acts of commercial coercion, the article from which the following extract is taken stresses the effect of Jeffersonian policy upon British exports, whereas most historians have been content to examine England's loss of supplies from America. Heaton begins by discussing the Nonimportation Act of 1806, which went into effect at about the same time as the embargo, and then notes that Secretary of the Treasury Albert Gallatin complained that large quantities of English goods were slipping into the United States despite these two policies*

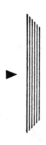

The Erosion of Economic Warfare

Gallatin stated only half the case when he referred to the increased temptations and habits of smuggling goods into the country. The Embargo had created a new temptation, to smuggle goods out. The fight against the latter has been well, but not completely, described by writers on the Embargo, and the general picture they have painted will probably only be amplified, rather than altered, by further research. The struggle against the smuggling of forbidden goods into the United States has not been studied, and records of the story are naturally scanty. There may have been some smuggling from the West Indies into New Orleans and the southeastern ports. Amelia Island, and St. Mary's River on the boundary between Georgia and Florida, may have been bases for inward as well as outward illicit traffic. Yet all the vessels seized on their return from embargo-breaking voyages to the West Indies are laden with molasses, sugar, and other island products, and none of them is caught with a bale of broadcloth.

In the north the story is different. British exports of manufactured goods to the

*Herbert Heaton, "Non-Importation, 1806-1812," *Journal of Economic History*, vol. I, no. 2 (November 1941), pp. 188-197. Reprinted with the permission of the *Journal of Economic History*

Maritime Provinces and the St. Lawrence or Lake Ontario regions increased by a quarter during 1808, and a further two thirds in 1809. With those areas there was the most active and the least repressible embargo-breaking, by sea to Nova Scotia or New Brunswick, and by raft, boat, cart, or sleigh from Maine, Vermont, and New York. The Embargo violations that found their way into court seem to have been chiefly one-way transactions; but there are evidences of imports as well. In July 1808, Gallatin wrote to at least two border collectors, urging them to be "on special guard," since he had heard that attempts were to be made to bring goods in from Canada; but he had been writing such letters ever since the two laws came into operation, and smuggling had been a normal by-occupation ever since the border was created. Few officials had the courage, or even perhaps the wish, to grapple with offenders, many of whom were ready to use violence if need be. Naval vessels had to be sent to the Maine coast, and regulars to upstate New York, while courts capable of dealing with seized goods were far from the frontier points. Records of some seizures have been found; for instance, Schenck [collector of customs at New York] in December detected a small shipment of woolens worth over 5/– a square yard, which had slipped in with a load of plaster of paris (a permitted import) from New Brunswick; and in November the collector at Albany laid hands on a bale of smuggled cloth, which was condemned and sold for over $1,200. But the impression remains nevertheless that laissez faire prevailed on the northern border.

It would, however, be foolish to assume that smuggling nullified either of the two prohibitive aspects of Jefferson's policy. As always, it was the fringe of

the shawl, a rather long fringe in places. But the smugglers could not develop enough resources in men or ships to take the place, or even a large part of the place, of the normal machinery of foreign trade. The ships and brigs which carried on the greater part of the transatlantic trade were in general tied up in obedience to the Embargo, or they went down the coast to load goods in readiness for the day when the light would change from red to green, and then returned to anchorage in their home ports. [Consul] Maury in Liverpool was not distressed by the arrival of a single embargo-breaker until late November, and was relieved then to find it was really a British ship. No American offender arrived till January 1809, and very few American vessels appeared in other European ports during 1808. Such merchants' letter books as have survived show little effort to indulge in large-scale defiance of the Embargo, at least until the end of 1808, when patience was becoming exhausted and repeal seemed inevitable. So far as the western hemisphere was concerned, smuggling and embargo-breaking could not be prevented; but against Europe the Embargo was largely effective. And if American ships did not go to Europe, British goods could not be brought back in them.

In view of these considerations, the surprising feature of the period is the substantial quantity of British goods that did enter the United States, and did so legally, during 1808. The American returns of imports are not very helpful, since the years run from October 1 to the following September 30; hence the figures for 1807-1808 begin with thirteen or fourteen weeks of free traffic; and in addition they do not give the value of goods that paid specific duties. The British export returns are more useful, since they deal with what are nearly calendar years. According to them, the "official" value of British goods sent to the United States fell from £7,740,000 in 1807 to £3,930,000 in 1808, a decline of 49 per cent; the "real" value dropped from £11,-850,000 to £5,240,000, or 55 per cent. To keep half of the United States market would seem an amazing achievement, especially when we remember that virtually all British goods were normally brought into the United States in American vessels.

Yet the explanation is not hard to find. By mid-June, when non-importation became effective, many American vessels that had left their home ports to winter in British harbors — a normal procedure even before threat of the Embargo made them and others scurry away in mid-December — had returned with unrestricted cargoes for the spring market. Some of these vessels usually made two round trips a year — westward, eastward, westward, eastward. The Embargo prevented them from making their second, third, and fourth journeys, and thus they could not make their contribution of British goods to the fall market. But a considerable number of American vessels did not return home till after June 14, and then came in with full cargoes of unobjectionable wares for the fall trade. On August 9, Maury wrote: "We still have American vessels for the United States, but the goods exporting thither prove so much beyond expectation that a sufficiency of American vessels could not be had, in consequence of which British [ships] are taken up and filling for various parts of the United States" at high freight rates.

This last sentence is a reminder that there was nothing in either the Embargo or Non-Importation Act to prevent British ships from bringing permitted goods; the only restriction on them was that they must leave American ports in ballast. This reduced their earning power, and their owners probably decided that they would be better employed on more profitable Canadian or West Indian routes, or in serving that newly opened El Dorado for British exports, Brazil and the Spanish American colonies. There is nevertheless some evidence, in addition to Maury's remark, that British vessels increased the quantity of goods carried lawfully by them to the United States.

By the end of 1808 it had become clear that partial non-importation was not proving fatal to British industry. Some branches of manufacture were being squeezed, but the pressure was not enough to make "the pips squeak," for escape was possible through increased exports to other parts of the western hemisphere. Meanwhile the Embargo was breaking down at the one point where it had been fairly effectively sustained. In every port, from New Orleans to Portland, scores of the larger ships were lying, crammed tight with American produce which they had either fetched from ports near the producing areas or had transshipped from coastal vessels. When Congress met in the fall, relief of some kind had been expected. Instead there came the ferocious amending act of January 9, 1809, which forced owners to unload their cargoes or give enormous bonds; and revenue officers came to seize sails, unship rudders, and place watchmen on wharves or decks. This was the last straw, and either directly or by subterfuge many ships made for the high seas. By the end of March, Maury had counted forty embargo-breakers in Liverpool, and expected many more. New York and New Jersey ports were the chief points of escape, but Savannah ran them a close second, and all the chief harbors of New

England, Virginia, and the Carolinas saw big birds fly away. It thus became evident that after a year's submission to the great, noble, grand, and sublime experiment, some shipowners and merchants in many places had suddenly and simultaneously decided to rebel.

All through the winter of 1808-1809 Congress was plagued by the question, "What next?" Plan One — partial non-importation — had ended without being given a fair trial. Plan Two — partial non-importation and complete embargo — had "promised so much and achieved so little" that it was economically and politically doomed. Two other plans remained to be tried, with an interlude between them. Plan Three was complete non-intercourse with the unrepentent belligerents, but free intercourse with the rest of the world. American ships could go anywhere except to British and French ports, whether home, colonial, or controlled. American ports were completely closed to British and French ships and goods, even if the latter came in neutral vessels. Thus partial non-importation was supplanted by a complete ban on *all* British goods, on all British *colonial* produce, and on all imports from the French Empire or occupied areas; while British and French ships were shut out as well. But the plan was baited with a promise of forgiveness in return for the abandonment of decrees or Orders-in-Council so far as they violated the neutral commerce of the United States.

The bait and the limited freedom granted to American ships bedeviled the whole plan. When the Embargo was lifted on March 15, and the merchantmen swarmed out, bonded and cleared for a "permitted" foreign port, obscure names suddenly loomed large in the list of destinations. Gothenburg, Tonningen, and other Scandinavian ports burst into popularity, and St. Bartholomew was inundated with spring cruisers. But for New Yorkers the greatest discovery was Fayal in the Azores. Not a single vessel had gone there in the second half of 1807, yet between March 15 and June 9 seventy-nine ships, all heavily laden, solemnly set sail for Fayal. In these strange places, the Americans might transfer their cargoes to British ships; but many of them did not waste time in that way. By May, Maury was complaining that "the non-intercourse violators are now coming in, and like the embargo-breakers they never come near my office." And by the end of 1809 most of the ships which had cleared for Fayal had returned from British ports. One of them was called *Madison*, another *Thomas Jefferson*.

Their return from British ports with British cargoes was made possible by the bait offered in the Non-Intercourse Act. In mid-April Erskine, British Ambassador in Washington, and Smith, the Secretary of State, reached an agreement, involving the abandonment of the Orders-in-Council so far as American ships were concerned. Thereupon Madison on April 19 proclaimed the end of non-intercourse with Britain on June 10, while Congress in June decreed that British ships and goods which had come in after full non-importation went into effect (May 20) were to be released from seizure and forfeiture. For the third time Schenck's seizures were restored. Hence many ships which cleared for permitted ports between April 19 and June 10 really intended to hover off the British coast and enter port on the tenth. Fifty of them came to anchor in Liverpool on the eleventh, and nearly as many during the next week. Fayal and Gothenburg were forgotten, and not a single vessel cleared New York for Fayal between June 10 and August 9.

Anglo-American trade boomed under that new deal. But that deal ended when in late July America heard that Canning had repudiated Erskine's agreement. On August 9, Madison declared non-intercourse was revived; but it was impossible to make this declaration effective at once. Ships that were in British ports or were bound there had to be permitted to come home laden with British goods, provided they used "all due diligence in returning." During the last four months of 1809, thirty-six ships reached Philadelphia from Britain; over a hundred arrivals in New York were recorded by the *Evening Post*. Hence America received an enormous supply of British wares during the fall; the "official" value of British exports to the United States rose nearly thirty per cent above the low level of 1808, and was about two thirds the pre-embargo figure. The "real" value rose nearly forty per cent, and was also two thirds that of 1807. The full effect of non-importation could not be seen until the spring of 1810, but on May 1 of that year non-intercourse expired. In his letters to collectors and his reports to Congress, Gallatin conveys his impression that smuggling from the north was more active than ever. The exports of British produce to Canada and the Maritimes jumped from £770,000 in 1808 to £1,272,000 in 1809.

On May 1, 1810, the interlude began when Congress [by Macon's Bill No. 2] let non-intercourse lapse, but threatened to revive part of it against either of the belligerents which did not follow suit if and when its enemy revoked the decrees or orders hurting American shipping. Napoleon promptly bamboozled Madison with a false declaration of the repeal of the obnoxious decrees. The news reached America in late September. Madison "declared" the repeal by a proclamation on November 2, 1810, and gave Great Britain three months in which to revoke her Orders-in-Council. Since she did not do so, she was subjected to a new brand of punishment on February 2, 1811. Business between May and the arrival of the French news was as buoyant in tone as in the days of the Erskine honeymoon in mid-1809. The open markets of the United States cheered the British, who were under a depressed aftermath of the South American boom of 1808-1809. The end of furtive contact with Britain cheered the Americans, who were also feeling the consequences of the British commercial collapse. Exports and imports, departures and arrivals, all climbed rapidly and drew near to those of 1807. American merchants mailed large orders to England, or went across to purchase goods on the spot. Britons swarmed to the United States to reëstablish or strengthen contacts, to pay or collect debts, or to settle down as members of one of the colonies of Scots, Lancashiremen, or Yorkshiremen that infested lower Manhattan.

This commercial convalescence was checked by the news from France and the President's proclamation; and as the months went by the lack of nourishing news from London caused a severe relapse. On February 2, 1811, Plan Four came into action. The new policy was not the old non-intercourse of 1809, but only half of it. By reviving nine clauses of the law of March 1, 1809, Congress forbade the entry of all British Empire ships and goods; but by leaving the other nine on the scrap heap it left American ships and goods free to go to Britain. It was thus at last a simple, complete, non-importation policy. Britain could buy, but not sell. She could import American produce in American ships, but not in

British bottoms. She could not send her goods to America, even in American vessels, and no neutrals could bring them as their own property. Even Napoleon could not devise a better plan for sapping an enemy's commercial and financial resources. The price for salvation was the repeal of the Orders-in-Council; once Madison heard that this had been done, he would proclaim the fact and the restrictions would immediately "cease and be discontinued."

This brand of non-importation lasted longer than any of its double-edged predecessors, and remained in force until war made British goods enemy products. It began with the usual muddle. Schenck and his fellow officers seized great quantities of goods which arrived soon after February 2, but Congress again belatedly provided a period of grace, and for the fourth time Schenck saw his efforts undone. Yet only a small fraction of the vast orders placed in 1810 had cleared British ports by February 2, and Congress would not allow the remainder to come in. Some British manufacturers or merchants had, on their own initiative, suspended the filling of these orders when they heard of the President's proclamation, while some American cancellations or suspensions had got through in time to hold up production or purchase. But great quantities of manufactures had been finished, packed, paid for, and dispatched to the ports in readiness for the spring sailings, and there they lay till the summer of 1812. To that mountain of bales, bundles, trusses, boxes, and crates, more were added during 1811 and early 1812 by Americans who thought they could discern a break in the clouds and were convinced that either Congress or the British Cabinet was going to relent. In addition, substantial orders were sent to every part of industrial Britain, to be filled as soon as there were certain signs that the Orders-in-Council were doomed. William Brown, a leading Anglo-American merchant, said that he had £100,000 of goods in his warehouse in the spring of 1812, and there were probably half a dozen firms that could have made the same statement.

To this heap of American goods, most of them bought and paid for, was added a rising pile of American credits from the sale of produce in England and on the Continent. The normal course of American transactions was to have most of the proceeds of sales on the Continent transferred to England, there to be drawn on for the purchase of British manufactures. Between 1805 and 1807 Great Britain sold two to three times as much to the United States as she bought from her. The most popular argument against the Orders-in-Council was that if Britain hindered the American sales to the Continent she would reduce this transfer of funds and thus impede the purchase of British industrial products. And a forceful but futile argument against Non-Importation was that if Americans could not buy from England they would not be able to repatriate the income they earned by selling on the Continent or in Britain, not to mention their shipping earnings.

During 1811 and early 1812 American exporters tried various makeshift ways of getting their property home. Some of them instructed their British agents to buy "stocks of the United States," Louisiana 6 per cents, securities of the liquidating first Bank of the United States, or any other kind of American bond that could be bought in London or Amsterdam. Some asked for bills or drafts, even though the price was high and the loss great. One shipowner wound up complicated instructions to his captain as follows: "If thou learn salt can be had at Cape de Verdes we think thee had best take specie enough with thee from England and proceed there and take a cargo for home." But bills and bonds, salt and specie, all were poor and inadequate substitutes for dry goods, pottery, and hardware. For their westward passages most vessels tried to earn a little money by fostering passenger traffic; but their holds were not even allowed to be filled with salable ballast, since coal and salt from Britain were forbidden entry. Gallatin's men were working hard, Schenck was in grand fighting form, and the Philadelphia collector was so strict that he hesitated long before allowing Irish immigrants to bring ashore their unconsumed stores of potatoes and oatmeal.

Smuggling played its part. Hezekiah Niles, never an expert in understatement, said that the Non-Importation Act was so ineffective that it should be called "An Act for the Better Encouragement of Roguery and Other Purposes." Gallatin admitted that some British rum and other commodities were coming in from non-British islands, and it was difficult to prove that it was British rum, even by calling experts into court to taste it. He agreed that prohibited goods were slipping in by sea and land from the north; but the whole situation was not serious. The evidence suggests that he was too complacent. The expanded British exports to Canada, the increased number of smugglers caught on the border, and information sent by the consul from London all indicate increased illicit activity. Many firms wished to have stocks of goods as near home as possible when surrender by Cabinet or Congress came. To have bales ready in Liverpool, Bristol, or London was wise; but to have them in Montreal, Quebec, Halifax, or Amelia Island was wiser. Washington Irving's firm quietly accumulated 150 casks of

hardware and glass in Montreal during the fall of 1811. John Jacob Astor built up a rich store of Canadian furs at St. Regis, a border point. Stephen .Girard and his associates landed three cargoes, worth at least $350,000, on Amelia Island during the winter of 1811-1812. If others built up such stocks, and then let some of them slip into the United States in anticipation of commercial emancipation, no one would be surprised, least of all Gallatin.

All these and similar devices could not make much impression on the mountain of goods in store or on order. The only way to break the dam was to force a political surrender in one of the two capitals. In January 1812, there were faint signs that Congress might relent so far as to allow Americans to bring in the goods they had *ordered* before February 2, 1811. Ships rushed eastward to gather them up, and Merseyside came to hectic life. But the signs faded away, and the war of nerves continued. More ships went to England to escape the Embargo imposed by Congress on April 4, 1812. Their arrival was an ominous indication of the temper in Washington. War must be coming, and only a revocation of the Orders-in-Council could save the day. To that end British manufacturers and merchants interested in the American market had already redoubled their efforts. This time they succeeded, and when the *London Gazette* of June 23 announced their victory they rushed into action with exuberance and zest. To each American customer every British exporter sent a letter, a circular, or a copy of the *Gazette*. Here is a typical one.

Sheffield, June 24, 1812.

Sir,

We have the pleasure to inform you that yesterday our Government issued a Declaration by which the British Orders-in-Council so far as they regard the United States of

America, stand revoked on the First Day of August next; and as the Non-Importation Law will then cease to operate, the Trade between the two Countries will be once more free from all obstructions.

We sincerely congratulate you on this happy event, and beg leave to assure you that every exertion in our power shall be made to forward the whole of your orders to Liverpool for Shipment, with the outmost possible dispatch.

We are, most respectfully,

Sir,

Your obliged Friends and Servants,
BAILEY, EADON & BAILEY.

The movement started by the revocation of the Orders gained speed and mass for three weeks before any hint of serious obstacles arrived from America, and official notification of the declaration of war did not arrive in England till the end of July. But even then there was no power, and certainly no will, to check the outrush of ships and goods. By the time the exports really petered out about the end of 1812, goods estimated to be worth £4,000,000 or nearly $20,000,000 had left British ports for the United States.

When, during the congressional session of 1811-1812, the decision was considered whether to substitute military action for commercial coercion, bellicose Westerners were often in the vanguard of prowar sentiment. Among the many historians who have sought to explain Western feeling is LOUIS M. HACKER, for many years a Columbia professor and dean, who has written many volumes on economic history as well as a biography of Alexander Hamilton. In the following article, Hacker argues that the West sought war so that the United States might acquire rich Canadian lands.*

The Desire for Canadian Land

What...is the certain way that can link the west with the war against England? Possibly it can be discovered if the assumption is accepted that the west as a sectional unit desired war for reasons peculiarly its own. Such a starting point having been conceded, certain preliminary observations may be made. In the first place, as far as the west, the articulate war-maker, was concerned, the freedom of the seas played only a minor part in the precipitation of the conflict. In the second place, it must be understood that the war of 1812 was really meant to be a land war, advocated and fought by a section of the country that had no contact with or interest in the things of the sea. That is to say, the war of 1812 was ordered by an agricultural people interested and sustained by the soil and was to have as its goal the acquisition of Canada not so much because that meant the cutting off of the living threat of England, as because Canada stood for great reserves of agricultural land. In short, the west desired Canada and therefore sought war with England. The elucidation of this point may furnish the key to the situation....

On the whole, [the West]...was an agricultural society without skill or resources. It committed all those sins which

*Louis M. Hacker, "Western Land Hunger and the War of 1812," *Mississippi Valley Historical Review*, vol. X (March 1924), pp. 366, 370-377, 387-389, 393-395. Reprinted with the permission of the *Mississippi Valley Historical Review* and the author.

characterize a wasteful and ignorant husbandry. Grass seed was not sown for hay and as a result the farm animals had to forage for themselves in the forests; the fields were not permitted to lie in pasturage; a single crop was planted in the soil until the land was exhausted; the manure was not returned to the fields; only a small part of the farm was brought under cultivation, the rest being permitted to stand in timber. Instruments of cultivation were rude and clumsy and only too few, many of them being made on the farm. It is plain why the American frontier settler was on the move continually. It was not his fear of a too close contact with the comforts and restraints of a civilized society that stirred him into a ceaseless activity, nor merely the chance of selling out at a profit to the coming wave of settlers; it was his wasting land that drove him on. Hunger was the goad. The pioneer farmer's ignorance, his inadequate facilities for cultivation, his limited means of transport necessitated his frequent changes of scene. He could succeed only with a virgin soil. That wasted, as far as he was concerned, and moving was an urgent necessity. Of course the reclamation of the land came through the more careful efforts of the second migratory wave. It was then that vegetables were grown, orchards were laid out, hemp was cultivated to be sold for conversion into cordage. But the pioneer had neither the patience nor the knowledge for any of these things.

The psychology of the farmer is therefore to be studied carefully in a consideration of the problems of this new region. The pioneers needed great tracts of land in order barely to sustain life. The hemp cultivator sought more fertile river bottoms for his product. Farmers of all classes wanted more land because it is one of the peculiar traits of an agri-

cultural society to expand unceasingly. In a rural community fields are the tangible signs of well-being and the individual farmer is never quite content with the limits of his domain. He must throw out the confines of his fence, even at the expense of his personal comfort and at the risk of his material safety. Land is the realest of property and the farmer treasures what he has and always longs for more. When, therefore, the policy of a nation is dictated by a pioneer and agricultural group, it is easy to see where the origins of a land-expansion policy lie. When one recalls that Porter came from the Genesee valley of New York, Clay and Johnson from the agricultural communities of Kentucky, the other western leaders of the war party in the twelfth congress from similar constituencies, the move on Canada in its major aspects becomes plain. Canada was agricultural land, lying in the basin of the St. Lawrence river, its rich bottom land still untouched by the plow. Canada in the nature of things was bound to tempt the agricultural west.

But what of the part of the Indian in the western life? It has been maintained steadfastly that it was the threat of a general Indian uprising coupled with British connivance from Canada that impelled the west into the war. What really did the figure of the Indian stand for? To the isolated community alone in the forests of Indiana or Illinois no doubt the Indian was a cause for vexation and, at many times, for plain dread. His silent figure, his unknown ways, his plainly perceptible loathing for his white neighbors who were encroaching on his hunting grounds, must often have brought forth expressions of a very real alarm. Yet instead of trying to understand the problem the pioneer conducted himself in a manner that was bound to feed further the hatred of the red man. Observers united in declaring that the pioneer regarded the Indian as an inferior creature no better than the beasts of the thicket. Indians were hunted down and coolly slain; the law officers never seriously took steps to bring the malefactors to justice. The right was never completely on one side; the Indians, rather, were more sinned against than sinning. With reason the threat of a general movement against the outlying settlements must have seemed a reality to the backwoodsmen. But, really, must not the problem be conceived in its larger terms? Should not the question be, not, were the Indians a menace to some isolated areas of settlement where both sides erred in their conduct, but, rather, did the Indians as a host threaten the existence of the white civilization in the Ohio valley? Conceived in such terms the Indian problem is shorn of its importance.

The number of Indians in the Ohio valley could never have been alarming. In Kentucky itself there was no threat of Indian danger. All the Indian lands except that part in the southwestern corner that lay in the bend between the Ohio and Tennessee rivers had already been preëmpted by this period. In Ohio in 1812 the Indians were scattered over about one-fourth of the area, mainly in the western and northern sections. Distributed over not quite six million acres were to be found in all 3,036 Indians of both sexes and all ages, divided into six principal tribes. The largest tribe, the Shawnee, had in all 840 people. The Wyandots, next in size, totaled 695 in all. The other tribes were numerically much smaller than these two. On the other hand, concentrated within the southern half of the state were to [be] found 230,760 whites, of whom 64,556 were males over twenty-one years of age.

In Illinois the tale was very much of a similar nature. A competent observer has recorded that the tribes were widely scattered and ranged over two-thirds of the whole state. Even if we should accept Henry Adams' rather large estimate of five thousand Indian warriors occupying the whole country stretching to the lakes and the Mississippi — of whom a considerable number belonging to the Sauk and Fox nations were unfriendly to the Shawnee people — we must recall that opposed to this array was a body of almost a million whites — most of them clustered about the Ohio and its waters — of whom at least one-fourth were men over twenty-one years of age and therefore capable of bearing arms. From the point of numbers it is difficult to see how the Indian danger could ever have been considered in a serious light. . . .

This is something of the scene into which it is necessary to project oneself before the war attitude of the west can be rightly understood. The people of the west, because of the nature of their lives, were accustomed to strenuous measures. War they regarded calmly. They felt no passion for England; they sensed no bonds of blood or religion. Here were to be found evidences of a fierce love of country that transcended any faint traces of a foreign kinship that may have remained. The inhabitants of the Ohio valley were for the most part of the second generation of pioneers. They had been too long removed from contact with the east or with Europe to feel the restraints of a common cultural heritage. What seemed to men like Josiah Quincy and John Randolph nothing short of fratricidal war, to Clay and Porter and Johnson was a just cause. The speech of Johnson in the house on December 11, 1811, was typical of the attitude of this new generation out of the west. The patriotism he voiced was a fiery creed, narrowly nationalistic in its conception. "Her [*England's*] disposition is unfriendly," he said: "her enmity is implacable; she sickens at our prosperity and happiness." The United States must be prepared to stand alone, proud of its achievements, glorying in its great future. "This foreign influence is a dangerous enemy; we should destroy the means of its circulation among us — like the fatal tunic it destroys where it touches. It is insidious, invisible — and takes advantages of the most unsuspecting hours of social intercourse." In this manner England was to be defied. "On to Canada," became the cry, and it was taken up by one after the other of the young westerners. . . .

With the meeting of the twelfth congress in 1811 the demand for the invasion and acquisition of Canada spread and grew until the whole Ohio valley reverberated with the idea. The lead was taken by the western members in the house and the newspapers were quick to follow. The statements are rather bald; one is not left long in the dark as to their purport. Felix Grundy of Tennessee struck the note in his speech of December 9, 1811, in the debate on the report of the foreign relations committee. "This war, if carried on successfully," he said, "will have its advantages. We shall drive the British from our Continent. . . . I therefore feel anxious not only to add the Floridas to the South, but the Canadas to the North of this empire." Johnson of Kentucky followed in the same vein: "I shall never die contended until I see her [*England's*] expulsion from North America and her territories incorporated with the United States. . . . In point of territorial limit the map will prove its importance [i.e., *the acqui-*

sition of Canada]. The waters of the St. Lawrence and the Mississippi interlock in a number of places and the Great Disposer of Human Events intended those two rivers should belong to the same people." Joseph Deshea [Desha] of Kentucky spoke calmly of his approval of the increase of the national force, for the "purposes intended, to wit, the subjugation of the British North American Provinces." And so it continued, again and again, the same plain sentiment turned over by many tongues, until John Randolph was forced to cry out: "Ever since the report of the committee on foreign relations came into the house, we have heard but one word — like the whip-poor-will, but one eternal monotonous tone — Canada! Canada! Canada!"

Randolph's scorn could hardly be expected to still the din. The Ohio valley newspapers became keenly inquisitive of Canadian affairs at this particular moment. At the same time, optimism over the success of a Canadian campaign ran unchecked. "It would be a short campaign to expel the British from the Canadas and Nova Scotia," quoted the Ohio *Muskingum Messenger* of November 20, 1811, from the *Kentucky Argus*. In the same issue the *Messenger* quite calmy asked for war. In its issue for April 4, 1812, this same paper also declared, "Our citizens ought therefore to be prepared for the last appeal of nations. — *WAR! WAR! WAR!*" On January 4, and on June 6, 1812, the *Lexington Reporter* (Kentucky) had stated that an attack on Canada would bring the war to a speedy close. In the latter number the editor had written, "Let every arm be nerved for the glorious contest; every voice prepared to bid it welcome! — England we can punish." A week later the same writer spoke confidently of the ease with which Canada could be made to capitulate.

That the citizens were in hearty accord with the sentiments of their editors and their representatives in congress may be gathered from that quaint organ for the expression of popular opinion, the formal dinner. The following toast, reported in a newspaper, must have been cheered to the echo, for it received seventeen huzzas: "May the starry flag of 1812 float triumphantly over the ramparts of Quebec." And this sentiment was greeted with thirteen cheers: "May the Twelfth Congress no longer tamely submit to British outrages, but wrest from her every foot of possession she holds in North America." The fourth of July dinners bubbled over with the same enthusiasm. Men of the Ohio valley drank to hopes such as these: "Canada — may it soon be counted as another star adorning our political hemisphere," and "The present Congress — the guardians of the nation. May their act of the eighteenth of June be crowned with immortal glory. . . ."

[While some Westerners no doubt advocated the conquest of Canada so that their British rivals would be driven from the fur trade with the Indians,] the chief preoccupation . . . must have been with those vistas of boundless Canadian lands. Randolph, by his insistence upon the fact, must have been convinced of its prominence among the motives guiding the men from the west. After listening to Grundy, Johnson, Calhoun, Deshea [Desha], and Troup, he could say openly: "Sir, if you go to war it will not be for the protection of, or defense of your maritime rights. Gentlemen from the North have been taken up to some high mountain and shown all the kingdoms of the earth; and Canada seems tempting

in their sight. That rich vein of Genesee land, which is said to be even better on the other side of the lake than on this [beckons to them]. Agrarian cupidity, not maritime right, urges the war. . . . Not a syllable about Halifax, which unquestionably should be our great object in a war for maritime security." Nor was anything said of Bermuda, he went on to point out. All the talk concerned itself with "this tit-bit Canada." He came back to the subject again and again in subsequent speeches. And then, seeing that his protests could be of no avail, he cried out in exasperation, "Are there no limits to the territory over which a republican government may be extended?" But there was no checking the young warhawks who had long before determined to try their wings. They were confident of their abilities, sure of themselves and their purpose. Calhoun, with more fire than he ordinarily displayed, voiced their aspirations when he said: "This is the second struggle for our liberty; and, if we do but justice to ourselves, it will be no less glorious and successful than the first. Let us but exert ourselves and we will meet with the prospering smile of Heaven. Sir, I assert it with confidence, a war just and necessary in its origin, wisely and vigorously carried on, and honorably terminated, would establish the integrity and prosperity of our country for centuries." It is no wonder that the more astute Randolph had referred on a previous occasion to the youthful Calhoun as that "gentleman of extensive experience."

The key to the desire for Canada is to be found in these utterances. Randolph had seen the traces of that "agrarian cupidity" which was undoubtedly a prime factor in coloring the purpose of the men in the west. Land was necessary for the development of an agricultural society and the Ohio valley turned to Canada for the replenishing of its supply. Why did it not look to the Mississippi and the lands beyond? Why did not the Ohio valley turn its eyes west instead of north? The question may well be asked, what of those great prairie tracts that, for millions of acres, swept unbrokenly across the center of the continent from northern Ohio to the edge of the Rocky mountains? The explanation of all these things lies in the fact that the prairies did not tempt the Ohio valley. In the clarification of this fact is centered the reason for the enthusiasm for Canada. The prairies, believed the pioneer and the farmer of the Ohio valley, could not be tilled because they were so far removed from the centers of communication, the rivers; because they did not furnish an adequate water supply for drinking and for the erection of mill seats; because they were unhealthful; and because they were bare of that natural element so important in the life of the farmer of the early nineteenth century — timber. Without standing timber the pioneer could not erect his rude log cabin and his barn; without timber the farmer was at a loss for material for his fences; and without timber neither the pioneer nor the farmer had fuel to make life supportable in the cruel winter months. In this primitive agricultural economy the presence of abundant wood was as important as the very soil itself. The railroads had first to make their appearance; coal had to be discovered in the Ohio valley; and wire had to be turned out for fencing, before the prairies could beckon to the settler. . . .

The general attitude toward the prairie land was summed up concisely and fairly enough by [a] . . . traveler, well known to the west. "Prevailing opinion," he wrote, "in regard to this portion of the country, viz. that it is unhealthy, appears too well-founded to admit of refutation." The stagnant waters collecting in pools on the prairies produce an "atmosphere that is humid and unhealthy. . . . The population of this region is limited. . . . Many parts of the country must remain uninhabited for many years to come, on account of the scarcity of timber and other deficiencies such as the want of mill-seats, springs of water, etc. which are serious blemishes in the character of a large proportion of the country."

In this attitude there is undoubtedly to be found the explanation of western interest in Canada. A pioneering society must always be on the move, but new lands are necessary, to which the pioneer, having sapped the soil, can turn. The lands of the prairies were in every sense undesirable. The Ohio valley must have read with keen interest, then, those accounts of the Canadian region which reached it. One may well imagine the hope that such a passage as the following aroused: "The country around Lake Ontario is almost everywheres extremely fertile, particularly that part which lies at the western end and on the Niagra River. Perhaps this is excelled by no part of the world. . . . The soil along Lake Erie is excellent and that of Huron and Superior is understood to be generally good. Perhaps no country on the globe could furnish such inexhaustible stores of ship timber as that which surrounds Lake Erie and Ontario." To the farmer this meant easy transportation, mill seats, abundant harvests, and fuel, fences, and farm buildings. If the United States was to have room for expansion, the proper direction for its energies was to the north. Let England only be defeated, and then Canada could be wrested from her. Here was a land to which one could move, a veritable farmer's paradise. Such, one may imagine, was assuredly the stuff of many a western farmer's dreams. There were some other motives set out for the conquest of Canada, but they were neither of any consequence nor possibly of much seriousness. The following, which may be taken as a sample of their import, is from the proclamation of General Andrew Jackson directed to the Tennessee volunteers: "Should the occupation of the Canadas be resolved upon by the general government how pleasing the prospect that would open to the young volunteer while performing a military promenade into a distant country! A succession of new and interesting objects would perpetually fill and delight his imagination, the effect of which would be heightened by the war-like appearances, the martial music and the grand evolutions of an army of fifty thousand men.

"To view the stupendous works of nature exemplified in the falls of Niagra and the cataract of Montmorena; and to tread the consecrated spot on which Wolfe and Montgomery fell, would of themselves repay the young soldier for a march across the continent. But why should these inducements be held out to the young men of America?" Is that not quite true? The west, long before the call to arms, had decided upon its war, for reasons which it alone understood. That the rest of the country was openly hostile was of no moment. The administration was to be bullied into a declaration, and the nation was to be armed for the encounter whether it willed it or no. War with England was the order of the day and Canada was the prize.

Within a year after the appearance of Hacker's article, it was answered in the same journal by JULIUS W. PRATT. Pratt was to become one of the leading American diplomatic historians, primarily on the strength of his studies of the expansionist movements of 1812 and 1898. While the article excerpted below is essentially a criticism of the Hacker theory, it clearly foreshadows the positive emphasis that Pratt was to offer in his book *Expansionists of 1812.**

The Land Hunger Thesis Challenged

At the very beginning of his discussion ..., Mr. Hacker falls into what I cannot help regarding as a fundamental error in psychology. "Should not the question be," he asks, "not, were the Indians a menace to some isolated areas of settlement where both sides erred in their conduct, but, rather, did the Indians as a host threaten the existence of the white civilization in the Ohio Valley? Conceived in such terms the Indian problem is shorn of its importance." Conceived in such terms most of the vexing problems of history would be shorn of their importance. Now and then comes a danger which actually threatens the existence of a nation or a people, but most international friction

and most wars arise from marginal irritations akin to that which existed in 1812 in the Ohio Valley. ...

No reasonable person would argue with Mr. Hacker when he shows that there was little danger of some 5000 Indian warriors wiping out settlements aggregating nearly 1,000,000 whites. But if the Ohio Valley had little cause for "wholesale fear" of the Indians, it does not follow that it did not feel wholesale detestation of them, and entertain a wholesale determination to render them harmless and punish any who aided them. Mr. Hacker himself pictures the Ohio Valley as possessing a cultural and psychological unity. Would not the center then feel the dangers existent upon

*Julius W. Pratt, "Western Aims in the War of 1812," *Mississippi Valley Historical Review*, vol. XII (June 1925), pp. 38-39, 43-50. Reprinted with the permission of the *Mississippi Valley Historical Review* and the author.

the periphery? There can hardly have been a family in the larger and older settlements which had not kinsmen on the border of the wilderness, where men thought of the Indian menace as a very personal matter. When Andrew Jackson wrote to Governor Harrison, after the battle of Tippecanoe, that "the *blood of our murdered countrymen must be revenged*," his words may have been a clever mask for his "land hunger"; I find it easier, however, to believe them the natural expression of a sentiment common to every man or woman with friends on the far frontier or in the militia. . . .

[Mr. Hacker states] that from 1808 to 1811 the village of Tecumseh and the Phophet was unmolested by the whites, and he draws the conclusion that the West's apprehension, whether real or feigned, developed suddenly in the latter year. This seems to Mr. Hacker to show that there was something artificial about this supposed apprehension. It is not necessary to examine the logic of this reasoning, for the facts . . . show that both the fear of the Indians and the habit of blaming the British for their hostile movements were widespread long before 1811. There was in 1810 and 1811 a sudden flaring up of anger against the Indians associated with Tecumseh and their supposed British backers. Why was it? Mr. Hacker cites numerous reports of outrages, murders, and the like which poured in to the government or blazed forth in the press. He apparently regards these as propaganda—the first move in the "secret policy of agrarian expansion." To me it seems simpler and more in accord with frontier psychology to regard them as based upon an actual increase in active Indian hostility.

As a matter of fact, the Prophet had been a subject of concern to Governor Harrison since 1807 at the latest, and the idea of taking Canada from the British as the only way of assuring peace with the Indians had been announced in Congress at the beginning of 1809. "By April, 1810," says Eggleston, the biographer of Tecumseh, "there was a general conviction on the part of the whites that the plans of Tecumseh and the Prophet were really hostile to the United States." In the summer and fall of that year, and throughout the year following, government officials, the western press, and resolutions of public meetings voiced their sense of danger and their conviction that the British were responsible for it. The climax came with the battle of Tippecanoe, November 7, 1811, in which Harrison's force suffered nearly two hundred casualties. It was then that Jackson called for vengeance for "the blood of our murdered countrymen" and the destruction of "this hostile band which must be excited to war by the secret agents of Great Britain." It was in the months immediately following that the war party in Congress proclaimed that the British must be driven from Canada, in order, in the words of Rhea of Tennessee, to "put it out of the power of Great Britain, or of any British agent, trader, or factor, or company of British traders to supply Indian tribes with arms or ammunition; to instigate and incite Indians to disturb and harass our frontiers, and to murder and scalp helpless women and children. It was on January 21, 1812 that the Lexington (Kentucky) *Reporter* published a *"Franklinian Prescription — To cure Indian hostilities, and to prevent their recurrence*: Interpose the American arm between the hands of the English and their savage allies."

. . . [T]his demand for the expulsion of the British from Canada, far from being a new and sudden development of western sentiment, was the perfectly logical culmination of a long contest with the Indians for the secure possession of the Northwest and of a conviction as old as the Revolution that the Indian resistance was supported by the British. If in 1812 it was a "lofty pretension" "masking a secret policy of agrarian expansion," this "lofty pretension" had been sedulously nurtured for thirty-five years.

Let us now examine Mr. Hacker's theory that the real motive of the West was the desire for possession of Canadian lands. "Pressing upon men's minds," he says, "was undoubtedly the picture of the good fat fields across the St. Lawrence River that ached for cultivation." What is the evidence? Mr. Hacker admits that "men never said so specifically." After a painstaking examination of western newspapers and the speeches of western congressmen, he is not able to adduce a single statement that these lands were needed or desired. This trifling weakness in the evidence is met by the suggestion that "possibly Westerners did not talk of those hopes nearest their hearts." Too astute to avow their "agrarian cupidity," they invented the British-Indian menace as a mask. On the face of it this suggestion seems to me untrue to frontier psychology; but fortunately we are not left in the dark about the Westerner's habit of concealing his material motives. If he studiously avoided all mention of farming lands as an object of war, why did he not also keep quiet about the fur trade? Was it more wicked, and hence more to be concealed, to covet Canadian lands than to covet the profits from Canadian furs? Yet the fur trade again and again creeps into war speeches and war articles. "Is it nothing to acquire the entire fur trade connected with that country?" Clay had asked in February, 1810. Grundy alluded to the same subject. Mr. Hacker himself cites an article published in the Muskingum *Messenger* in August, 1812, which he calls "the only coherent attempt on the part of any western paper to enumerate the reasons why Canada ought to be taken"—an article which makes no mention of lands but is plain enough about the fur trade. In the face of these avowals, it is difficult to see why Mr. Hacker should characterize Johnson's statement on the same subject as taking place "in an unguarded moment."

In the Southwest, furthermore, where certain material gains were distinctly sought, there was no pretense of excluding them from discussion. Tennesseeans were perfectly frank about stating their cupidity for the waterways of West Florida, and did not hesitate to picture the opportunities for wealth which American conquerors might enjoy in Mexico, "where the merchant shall see commercial resources unrivalled in other countries; the farmer, a luxuriant soil and delicious climate, where the financier shall be dazzled with gold and silver mines."

It seems highly probable, that if the Ohio Valley had been chiefly preoccupied with "vistas of boundless Canadian lands," some newspaper or public speaker would have disclosed this motive. In the absence of any direct evidence from Westerners themselves, Mr. Hacker bases his theory upon two foundations: the charges of John Randolph in Congress, and the argument, painstakingly built up, that the people of the Northwest supposed the good lands of the United States to be nearly all utilized.

John Randolph made several speeches during the winter of 1811-12, in which he denounced the war-makers. In one of these he referred sarcastically to "that rich vein of Gennesee land, which is said to be even better on the other side of the lake than on this," and declared that "agrarian cupidity, not maritime right, urges the war." This and other similar utterances of Randolph, thinks Mr. Hacker, give us "the key to the desire for Canada."

Even were Randolph's assertions all consistent, we might be pardoned for giving them slight consideration. His unscrupulous abuse of men and measures he disliked is well known to students of American history. No one believes, because Randolph said so in 1826, that John Quincy Adams "had selected for his pattern, the celebrated Anacharsis Cloots," that "as Anacharsis was the orator of the human race, so Adams was determined to be the President of the human race." Randolph's hatred for the Westerners—"Clay, Grundy, & Co.," as he dubbed them—was quite as intense as for Adams, and we might therefore at best take his charges against them with a grain of salt.

But Randolph's charges were not even consistent. At one time it was "agrarian cupidity" that urged the war; at another, it was the prospective war profits of the hemp-growers or of those who expected to furnish supplies for the troops; at yet another it was the desire on the part of the northern states "to acquire a prepondering northern influence." It is reasonably evident that Randolph was intent on using any taunt that might sting his opponents or divide their following. To seize upon one of these taunts, ignoring the others, and designate that one as "the key to the desire for Canada," is about as weak a form of historical argument as can be imagined—unless, of course, the charge selected has strong corroboration elsewhere.

The only corroboration offered by Mr. Hacker is drawn from the nature of pioneer agricultural economy and the low value at that time ascribed to prairie lands. Wasteful and inefficient methods of agriculture resulted in rapid exhaustion of the soil, and forced the advance guard of settlement to be constantly on the move, leaving their deteriorated soil to be reclaimed by methods more expensive and laborious. The question might be raised whether the resulting forward pressure was, in 1811-12, quite as urgent as Mr. Hacker assumes, but we may grant that western society was determined to continue its expansion. But why should the Ohio Valley have "turned to Canada for the replenishing of its supply" of land? Because says Mr. Hacker, "the prairies did not tempt the Ohio Valley," and he then details the numerous difficulties which were supposed to impede prairie agriculture. . . .

The weakness of this portion of the argument lies in the assumption that only treeless plains remained unoccupied. A comparison of the census made for 1810 with a map exhibiting the native vegetation of the country shows a vast area of timbered land as yet unpeopled—a third of the state of Ohio, nearly all of Indiana, and fringes of Illinois timbered with hardwood; all of Michigan, Wisconsin, and much of Minnesota bearing hardwood or pine; a great hardwood belt averaging one hundred miles in breadth stretching across Missouri into Arkansas and Oklahoma, with a narrow belt following the Missouri River across the state. John Bradbury, who made a journey through the West in 1809-11, and of whose *Travels in the Interior of America* Mr. Hacker makes use, describes a lightly-timbered belt extending westward 200 miles from the Mississippi River before the treeless plains began. Missouri Territory, he thought, was unsurpassed by any part of the western country in the advantages offered to settlers. Not only could land be easily obtained, but much of the ordinary labor of clearing a plantation could be avoided, "as here the trees are not more abundant on the upland than would be necessary for fuel and fences"; and he added another advantage: "This country, as well as the western region, will reap incalculable benefit from the application of steam boats on the Mississippi. Of these a great many are now building in the different ports of the Ohio. This mode of conveyance will also be much facilitated by the abundance of excellent coal so universally spread over these regions."

Bradbury wrote also a description of another western area which the land-hungry settlers had still before them. The northern parts of Ohio and Indiana (to which he erroneously added the whole of Illinois) consisted of "an assemblage of woodland and prairie . . . with the aggregate area of the prairie exceeding that of the woodland in the proportion of three or four to one." Bradbury considered this area the best part of the United States, with the exception of Upper Louisiana (Missouri). He explained how the settler, by placing his dwelling at the edge of a prairie, could have at once unlimited feed for his cattle, timber for house, fences, and fire, and land reducible at once to a state of tillage. It was his opinion that but for its greater distance from the Alleghenies than the heavily wooded region, this land "would undoubtedly have been the first settled."

It would appear, then, that the Ohio Valley was not in such desperate straits for land that it must deliberately inaugurate a war of agrarian expansion. The absence from the literature of the war of all mention of those "good fat fields across the St. Lawrence" as one of the objects of the conflict, is best explained by the simplest of all reasons — namely, that there were plenty of "good fat fields" at home. At the same time, if the inferences of this article have been correctly drawn, the Northwest was in reality intensely preoccupied with the Indian danger on its borders and the British hostility thought to be lurking behind it. In other words, we must believe that when newspapers and political leaders almost universally talked about Indians and British they meant what they said, and were not adroitly concealing their real interests.

Indirectly, of course, "agrarian cupidity" was at the root of the trouble. If the war spirit in the Northwest grew out of friction with the Indians, that friction was in turn the product of the American expansion into the Indian lands. If the whites had not coveted the lands of the Indians, possibly even if they had gone about getting them by more moderate and fairer means, Indian hostility might have been avoided and with it the "British-Indian menace." But it is only in this indirect sense that "agrarian cupidity" can be said to have been the actuating motive of the West in its demand for war, and this is not the sense in which the term was used by John Randolph and accepted by Mr. Hacker.

Less than a year after replying to Hacker, Pratt published his own interpretation of war sentiment in the South and West. A warning, in the preface, that he was dealing with "one set of causes only" was ignored by many readers who sought a simple explanation for the coming of war. In *Expansionists of 1812*, JULIUS PRATT repeated, often using the same evidence that he had mobilized against Hacker's Canadian theory, the arguments showing Western concern over the Indians; only a small portion of this analysis is reprinted here. Pratt then went on to describe Southern ambitions to absorb Canada and to suggest that a bargain was struck between South and West to achieve their respective ends.*

► *The Bargain between South and West*

Throughout the year 1811, alarm at the menace of Tecumseh's confederacy and conviction that the British were instrumental in its formation and support grew rapidly among government officials and the people of the West. Governor Harrison [of the Indiana Territory] wrote in February to the Secretary of War: "If the intentions of the British Government are pacific, the Indian department of Upper Canada have not been made acquainted with them: for they have very lately said every thing to the Indians, who visited them, to excite them against us."

In July a group of citizens of Knox County, Indiana, met at Vincennes and adopted resolutions demanding that the Indian settlement at Tippecanoe — one hundred and fifty miles up the Wabash — be broken up. The wish was natural, in view of the serious menace which the Prophet's town held over the heads of the Knox County settlers; but it was significant that the British were charged with responsibility for the whole situation. "We are fully convinced," said the resolution, "that the formation of the combination, headed by the Shawanee prophet, is a British scheme, and that

*Julius W. Pratt, *Expansionists of 1812*, New York, 1925, pp. 43-52. 54-60, 120-122, 125-130, 134-135, 138-143, 147-152. Reprinted with the permission of Peter Smith, Inc., publishers.

the agents of that power are constantly exciting the Indians to hostilities against the United States. . . ."

Meanwhile the *Kentucky Gazette* was warning its readers of the British-Indian menace in outspoken language:

"It would seem from the attitude of the Indians — the combination of the Northern and Southern tribes — the conference at Malden — the circumstances attendant on the mission of *Foster* — the late arrival of regular troops in Canada, that the British ministry were planning '*another expedition.*' . . .

"From the friendly course pursued by Mr. Jefferson, towards our red neighbors, and which has been followed by Mr. Madison, we had supposed the Indians would never more treat us otherwise than as brethren. But we have been mistaken — British intrigue and British gold, it seems, has greater influence with them of late than American justice and benevolence. . . . We have in our possession information which proves beyond doubt, the late disturbances to be owing to the too successful intrigues of British emissaries with the Indians."

Governor Harrison, representative of "American justice and benevolence" toward the Indians, was at this time planning to open the way to a military career by an attack on the Indian village at Tippecanoe. But he knew that war with England was probable, and suspected that the regiment of regular troops now on their way to him from Pittsburgh, were destined "to our frontiers bordering on Upper Canada." More important than his own ideas on the subject was his estimate of the spirit of the western people, whom he knew if any one knew them. "The people of this Territory [Indiana] and Kentucky," he wrote, "are extremely pressing in offers of their service for an expedition into the Indian

Country. Any number of men might be obtained for this purpose or for a march into Canada."

Early in September it was reported to Harrison "that defection is evidenced amongst all the Tribes from the Wabash to the Mississippi and the Lakes. That the Indians of the Wabash, Illinois, etc., have recently visited the British agent at Malden. That they are now returning from thence with a larger supply of goods than is ever known to have been distributed to them before. That rifles or fusees are given to those who are unarmed and powder and lead to all. And that the language and measures of the Indians indicate nothing but war." Harrison passed on the information to the War Department a few days later (September 17, 1811), with additional details of the extent of British subsidies: "A trader of this country was lately in the King's store at Malden, and was told that the quantity of goods for the Indian department, which has been sent out this year, exceeded that of common years by £20,000 sterling. It is impossible to ascribe this profusion to any other motive than that of instigating the Indians to take up the tomahawk; it cannot be to secure their trade, for all the peltries collected on the waters of the Wabash, in one year, if sold in the London market, would not pay the freight of the goods which have been given the Indians."

Harrison, however, went on to say that, "although I am decidedly of opinion that the tendency of the British measures is hostility to us, candor obliges me to inform you, that, from two Indians of different tribes, I have received information that the British agent absolutely dissuaded them from going to war against the United States." That the compulsion of candor was necessary to bring the governor to pass on this last bit of information is an interesting commentary on his state of mind; but the information itself is perfectly consistent with the other facts of the situation. General Brock wrote, after Harrison's battle with the Indians, that the latter had been "implicitly told not to look for assistance from us," but the phrase occurs in a letter whose main purpose was to point out how the effective aid of the Indians was to be secured and used against the Americans. Throughout the period of the rise of Tecumseh, the British had dissuaded the Indians from beginning a war against the United States; but the purpose of this policy was to allow time for the consolidation of the confederacy, that the aid of the Indians might be the more effective when needed.

Early in November came Harrison's badly managed campaign ending in the battle of Tippecanoe. From the facts already presented it is clear that the blood there shed would be added to the grievances already existing against the British and would bring the West to an eagerness for war without precedent in the entire controversy. "The *blood of our murdered countrymen must be revenged,*" wrote Andrew Jackson to Harrison. "I do hope that Government will see that it is necessary to act efficiently and that this hostile band which must be excited to war by the secret agents of Great Britain must be destroyed." The battle of Tippecanoe gave inestimable support to the war party in the Twelfth Congress, now assembled in Washington for its first session.

The war party, composed of western men and "radical, expansionist, malcontent politicians of the east," which had existed in Congress since 1810 at least, found itself in full control when the Twelfth Congress met. Clay, the most prominent of the "war hawks," came now to the House of Representatives, where he was at once chosen speaker. He was supported in his warlike policy by members from the frontier sections of the northern states, such as Peter B. Porter of New York and John A. Harper of New Hampshire; by almost the entire delegation of the western states —Worthington of Ohio and Pope of Kentucky, both in the Senate, were the only important exceptions — by a fair proportion of the members from Pennsylvania, Virginia, and North Carolina; and by a very able and aggressive group of young men from South Carolina and Georgia — Calhoun, Cheves, Lowndes, Crawford, Troup, and others — men who had reasons of their own for promoting a war of expansion.

It was soon apparent that the war to which this party was committed was to be no such purely defensive war as the Tenth Congress had contemplated, but that it was to be waged aggressively and with the conquest of Canada as a major object. Some Easterners might agree with Monroe that Canada might be invaded, "not as an object of the war but as a means to bring it to a satisfactory conclusion," but the West was more of the mind of a correspondent of the Philadelphia *Aurora*, "who wrote that if England were to restore all impressed seamen and make compensation for all her depredations we should listen to no terms that did not include Upper Canada."

President Madison's annual message, delivered to Congress on November 5, contained language that could plainly be interpreted as meaning war. After touching upon the obdurate persistence of Great Britain in attacking American commerce, he went on to say: "With this evidence of hostile inflexibility, in trampling on rights which no independent nation can relinquish, Congress will feel the duty of putting the United States into an armor and an attitude demanded by the crisis, and corresponding with the national spirit and expectations." To deal with that part of the message concerned with foreign relations, Speaker Clay appointed a select committee, upon which he placed a group of the most reliable war men — Porter, Calhoun, Grundy, Harper, and Desha. The committee reported on November 29 a set of six resolutions recommending an increase of ten thousand men for the regular army, a levy of fifty thousand volunteers, the outfitting of all vessels of war not in active service, and the arming of merchant vessels.

It was in the House debate on these resolutions that the war party frankly revealed their designs upon Canada. Mr. Porter, chairman of the committee, speaking on December 6, explained that in addition to the injury which American privateers could inflict upon British commerce, "there was another point where we could attack her, and where she would feel our power still more sensibly. We could deprive her of her extensive provinces lying along our borders to the north. These provinces were not only immensely valuable in themselves, but almost indispensable to the existence of Great Britain, cut off as she now in a great measure is from the north of Europe. He had been credibly informed that the exports from Quebec alone amounted during the last year, to near six millions of dollars, and most of these too in articles of the first necessity — in ship timber and in provisions for the support of her fleets and armies. By carrying on such a war as he had described ... we should be able in a short

time to remunerate ourselves tenfold for all the spoliations she had committed on our commerce."

Grundy of Tennessee, three days later, dwelt upon the peculiar advantage to the Westerner to be derived from war. "We shall drive the British from our Continent — they will no longer have an opportunity of intriguing with our Indian neighbors, and setting on the ruthless savage to tomahawk our women and children. That nation will lose her Canadian trade, and, by having no resting place in this country, her means of annoying us will be diminished." Rhea of Tennessee was equally explicit upon the object of the war —"That all that part of North America which j·.ns the United States on the Northeast, North, and Northwest, shall be provided for in a mode which will forever thereafter put it out of the power of Great Britain, or of any British agent, trader, or factor, or company of British traders to supply Indian tribes with arms or ammunition; to instigate and incite Indians to disturb and harass our frontiers, and to murder and scalp helpless women and children. . . ."

The West no longer needed any such promptings from its representatives in Washington. The rise of Tecumseh and the Prophet, the battle of Tippecanoe, the outspoken position of their congressmen, together with the current belief that the British were behind all their Indian troubles, had resulted in an insistent demand from the Westerners for the conquest of Canada. The Lexington *Reporter* published in January a *"Franklinian Prescription — To cure Indian hostilities, and to prevent their recurrence:* Interpose the American arm between the hands of the English and their savage allies. This done, the occupation of **the**

Canadas, New Brunswick and Nova-Scotia, would give us perpetual concord with the Indians; who would be obliged *to depend upon us* for supplies of Blankets, knives, gun-powder, etc."

The Kentucky Legislature, which in the crisis of 1807-1808 had made no official mention of the border question, in its resolutions of February, 1812, added to Great Britain's violations of American rights at sea her practice of "inciting the savages (as we have strong reasons to believe) to murder the inhabitants of our defenceless frontiers — furnishing them with arms and ammunition lately, to attack our forces; to the loss of a number of our brave men."

Another indication of public opinion in Kentucky is the character of the toasts proposed at a Washington's Birthday dinner in Lexington. The banqueters drank to such toasts as *"Great Britain, when she comes to her senses —* If she continues lunatic, *Canada* and our arms!" or *"The American Congress —* If they barter the nation's honor under the false idea of temporary popularity, may they meet with the just scorn of an indignant people!"

Public opinion in Ohio paralleled closely that of Kentucky. The Circleville *Fredonian* declared the "indignant spirits" of Americans could be appeased only "by the restoration of our rights, or the conquest of Canada." Correspondents of Senator Thomas Worthington believed that if war came, "we would attack [and] conquer Cannady & humble their overbearing pride," or hoped that American troops would "sever Upper Canada from the British without delay."

As the year advanced, the tone of the press grew even more determined. The *Fredonian* saw no hope of peace and security from the savages until "another

WAYNE shall force *them* to become our friends, and another WASHINGTON exterminates from the Canadas, the base remains of royal perfidy." The British "must be for ever driven from all their possessions in America." The same paper professed itself eager to undertake a war against both France and Great Britain when it appeared that neither nation was willing to recognize American rights. In April the *Kentucky Gazette* stated: "Great Britain has determined not to recede, and Congress seem at last to have got in earnest, and appear disposed to prepare for war.... The recruiting service has been actually commenced in various places, and large bodies of militia are to be raised to march for Detroit and other parts of our frontier. This is all preparatory to the invasion of Canada, now more than ever necessary, as presenting whilst in the possession of Britain, a never failing source of Indian hostility. Until those civilized allies of our Savage neighbors, are expelled from our continent, we must expect the frequent recurrence of the late scenes on the Wabash."

The same paper could not suppress its wrath when the *National Intelligencer*, reputed to be the administration organ, hinted that war might yet be avoided. "Notwithstanding a mass of evidence of this kind [i. e. as to captures, impressment, Henry plots, etc.], the Intelligencer may talk of *negociation* and '*honorable accommodation*' with England; but when we view of the effects of her policy in the *West* — when we hear of the tragic scenes that are now acting on our frontiers, after the slaughter of Tippecanoe, it is really surprising to hear that there is any doubt about the '*active preparations for warlike operations*' ... We will only add, at this time, that we should much like to know the price which the 'Intelligencer' would receive as a compromise for the scalps of *Western Farmers.*"

On May 26, three weeks before the declaration of war, the *Gazette* gave what appears like a parting injunction to Congress: "Can it be expected that those savage butcheries will have an end until we take possession of Malden and other British forts on the Lakes? And must the settlements in our territories be entirely destroyed, and the blood of the women and children drench the soil before this can be done?...What will our Congress say?" In similar tone the *Reporter* of May 30 declared: "Britain has commenced war in the Western Country, equally so as France would have done, was she to burn New York. The citizens of the Eastern States, and members in Congress, may abandon 7,000 seamen — they may term it, a *trifling impropriety* on the part of England, but the old Revolutionary Heroes here are not to be deceived by the misrepresentations of any man whatever. The Government MUST not abandon the Western Country to the British."

Thus by the end of the spring of 1812, the whole frontier country from New Hampshire to Kentucky was insisting that the British must be expelled from Canada. The demand had been of slow growth. Taking its origin from the ideas of Revolutionary statesmen, it was fed from various sources — from jealousy of the British fur trade, from exasperation at British contempt for the American flag at sea, from the alluring vision of a continent destined to recognize a single sovereignty — but unquestionably most of all from the conviction that the British in Canada were in unholy alliance with the western Indians, and that only by cutting off the Indians from British sup-

port could the West gain peace and security. Only thus could the Westerner be free to continue that policy of "justice and benevolence" toward the Indians, which consisted in pushing the boundaries of the white settlements ever farther into the Indian country. Other motives — commercial, political, punitive — played a part; but the overmastering desire of the people of the Northwest was to feel free to develop their country without peril from those Indian conspiracies which were universally believed to have their origin in British Canada.

If the Northwest, from 1783 to 1811, had harbored a suppressed desire for Canada, the Southwest had found it either impossible or unnecessary to suppress entirely its passion for the Spanish provinces. At first Florida and Louisiana, and after 1803 Florida and Mexico, had been the goals to which the ambitious turned their eyes, and scarcely a year had passed without some attempt by restless frontiersmen to subvert Spanish rule in some portion of His Catholic Majesty's dominions. Here land and the control of transportation routes had been the principal aims of the expansionists, but with these had been mingled other motives — the dread of Spanish influence among the Indians, the fear that Florida might be used by Spain or some other power as a base of operations against the United States, and the desire to secure full control of the Gulf of Mexico....

The demand for the annexation of all Florida was more insistent than ever [in 1812]. Georgians like Floyd, Mitchell, Troup, and Crawford — the last two influential members of the war party in Congress — held the acquisition of East Florida essential to the prosperity, to the very safety, of their state. The Augusta *Chronicle* ... hoped for "some new measures for the purpose of placing the whole of that colony under the control of the United States." Out in Mississippi Territory, the news of the occupation of East Florida aroused a lively hope of similar action farther west. . . .

But if the whole southern border was eager to take what remained of Florida, war with England seemed to afford a perfectly clear' occasion for doing so. Spain was England's ally in the European war, and it was safe to assume that Spanish harbors in America would be open to British fleets and armies. As a simple measure of self-defense, the occupation of Florida seemed to many indispensable, and it was commonly assumed at the South that war with England meant war with Spain, or at least the forcible occupation of all Florida.

. . . Expansionists like Clay and Harper, when they hurled defiance at Great Britain, had spoken in one breath of the nation's prospective conquests on the St. Lawrence and the Gulf of Mexico. Grundy of Tennessee, in the war debate in December, 1811, stated that he felt anxious "not only to add the Floridas to the South, but the Canadas to the North of this empire." and he wrote to Jackson that in case of war "the Canadas & Floridas will be the Theatres of our offensive operations."

Jackson himself, when shortly after the declaration of war he called upon his division of Tennessee militia to be in readiness, assured them that it was in West Florida that their arms should find employment. Jefferson, writing of the mustering of the militia in his Virginia county in June, 1812, said that "the only inquiry they make is whether they are to go to Canada or Florida. . . ."

Thus while the Northwesterner expected to take Canada as a result of war with Great Britain, southern men generally expected to complete the seizure of Florida from Great Britain's ally, Spain, while the more ambitious expansionists of the Southwest dreamed of further aggressions upon the Spanish territories, which should end in making the United States co-extensive with the continent of North America.

If we should locate on a map of the United States the homes of those men in Congress who were most outspoken for war and annexation, and plot from these points the line of maximum war and expansionist sentiment, we should find our line to be the circumference of a crescent with one end in New Hampshire and the other in Savannah, Georgia. Beginning with John A. Harper in the former state, we should pass westward through the home of Peter B. Porter, near Buffalo, New York, thence southwestward through the country of Clay and Johnson in Kentucky, Grundy and Campbell in Tennessee, down through the Abbeville section of South Carolina, the home of Calhoun, and finally to Savannah, in the district represented by George M. Troup. From end to end the crescent traversed frontier territory, bordering foreign soil, British and Spanish, or confronting dangerous Indian tribes among whom foreign influence was suspected and feared. And the men who came from these districts to Washington displayed many of the characteristic frontier traits. They had national patriotism, to the point sometimes of chauvinism, resenting with a new bitterness their country's wrongs and scorning the pacific measures hitherto used to repel them. They had unlimited faith in their country's future, believing its destined limits to be no less than the eastern and western oceans, the Gulf of Mexico and the "regions of eternal frost." Hence they were for a war which should at the same time defend the country's rights and expand its boundaries; they would punish British insults with the sword, wresting Canada from Great Britain and the residue of the Floridas from her weak ally, Spain.

Nothing could better demonstrate the frontier character of the war spirit than to observe its progressive decline as we pass from the rim of the crescent to its center at the national capital. Expansionist enthusiasm declined even more rapidly. Thus Cheves and Lowndes of South Carolina, Charlestonians both, were good war men but felt little interest in expansion even at the south. In New York, the two senators, Smith from Long Island, and German from a midstate county, though both Republicans, voted frequently with the anti-war party; German eventually voted against the declaration of war. A step nearer to Washington we have, on the south, Stanford of North Carolina and Randolph of Virginia in the House and Giles of Virginia in the Senate; on the north, Samuel Smith of Maryland and Michael Leib of Pennsylvania, both in the Senate — a group of Republicans who perhaps did more than the Federalists to embarrass the government in its war measures. Randolph was on principle opposed to war with Great Britain and had only contempt for talk of annexing Canada. Stanford apparently took his views from Randolph. But the Senate clique composed of Giles, Samuel Smith and Leib formed a faction whose ruling principle, if we may believe Henry Adams, was their hatred of Gallatin, and whose course in Congress was shaped more with a view to embarrassing the Treasury than to serving the interests of their country. Leib and his friend, Duane, publisher of the Philadelphia *Aurora,* had quarrelled with Gallatin long before

over the the patronage; Smith, over the administration of the Navy Department by his brother, Robert Smith. The exact cause of Giles's hatred of Gallatin is not clear, but it was whispered that he resented Madison's failure to make him (Giles) Secretary of State or to send him on an important foreign mission. He was described as "deadly hostile to Mr. Monroe, and not much in *love* with Mr. Madison."

These men, representing points far distant from the frontier, formed the nucleus of the anti-administration faction in the Senate. They were on occasion reinforced by Senators from nearer the border. German of New York had affiliations with the group, and his colleague Smith sometimes voted with them. Gilman of New Hampshire had covertly opposed Madison's election and could not be counted on to support the administration. Governor Plumer had no confidence in his Republicanism. More surprising was the defection of two western senators, Worthington of Ohio and Pope of Kentucky. Worthington, as his dairy shows, was little impressed by reports of British intrigues among the Indians; he deplored the horrors of war and saw its approach with grave misgivings. He had, moreover, changed his politics several times, and his allegiance to the Republican party was thought to be insecure. Pope, singularly enough, had described himself four years before as a straight administration man, standing high both "on the score of talents and Republicanism," and had added that "except Breckenridge no man from the West ever had more popularity in Congress...." He now generally worked with the Giles clique. Both Pope and Worthington were out of touch with Republican sentiment in the states they represented.

As there were men from the border who opposed the war, and cared nothing for territorial expansion, so there were men from the older states and districts who warmly supported both. Macon of North Carolina and Matthew Clay of Virginia, and a considerable part of the Pennsylvania delegation showed unquestioned zeal for the war program and the annexation of Canada. In general, however, our thesis holds good — that enthusiasm for war and annexation was at its height at the periphery of the crescent, while faction flourished most luxuriantly near the center. . . .

It is thus apparent that the nation in 1812 was divided by a two-fold cleavage. There was, first, the line between East and West, or more accurately, between the frontier crescent from New Hampshire to Georgia, and the more settled and stable portions of the country. Here war men and annexationists, all Republicans, were opposed, in the north by New England Federalism, and in the Middle States, from New York to North Carolina, by the factious and anti-war Republicans with a scattering of Federalists. Cutting across this line at right angles was a second line of cleavage between the commercial and the planter states, the free and the slave states. In terms of bitterness and distrust, this line cut far deeper than the first. Between East and West there might be disagreement in interests and ideals; between New England Federalism and Southern Planterdom there was implacable enmity. Thus the Federalists formed the nucleus for a sectional Northern party. How real was the tie that bound northern Republicans to their political allies in the South?

Up to the winter of 1812 northern Republicans had as a rule supported southern policies. The enabling act for Or-leans territory had been opposed by only three Republicans in the Senate — Gilman of New Hampshire, German of New York, and Reed of Maryland — and one in the House — Van Rensselaer of New York. The bill for the occupation of Florida had received even fuller support, Reed of Maryland casting the only northern Republican vote against it. On these measures, too, the few southern Federalists had voted with their New England colleagues. . . .

[However, the congressional reapportionment made necessary by the third United States census provoked debate that threatened to divide the Republicans along sectional lines. Were slave or free state to have a predominate share of power? This debate cast a shadow over the expansionist aims of both sections.]

If . . . there was developing a sectional consciousness which could on occasion transcend the older partisan lines, allying Federalists and Republicans of either section against the other; if political leaders of each section, regardless of party, distrusted any addition to the power of the other, it would seem natural that northern and southern Republicans should have viewed differently the programs of territorial expansion now before the country. Would not northern Republicans, though till now they had supported the occupation of Florida and the admission of new states in the southwest, fear the additional power that such measures would eventually give the South? And, on the other hand, could a southern Republican like Grundy, who opposed an appropriation for the "New York Mammoth Canal" because, as he wrote Jackson, by such a measure "no other purpose could be answered except to increase the power of the Northern Section of the Union," favor wholeheartedly the annexation of Canada, which would mean eventually the addition of several northern states? Kentuckians, perhaps, might wish with equal zeal for expansion north and south, for Kentucky was at once so southern as to feel a vital interest in the river outlets to the Gulf, and so northern as to be tragically alive to the dangers arising from British manipulation of the Indians of the Northwest. But the states north and northeast of Kentucky could hope to receive no benefit, and must see a political danger, in annexing Florida, while the states to the south and southeast must feel a similarly lukewarm interest in the annexation of Canada.

If, however, the two measures could go hand in hand, and Canada and Florida be at once added to the national domain, then the expansionists of both sections could fulfill their hopes, and the balance of power would remain substantially unchanged. When, therefore, we find southern men advocating the conquest and annexation of Canada, we may suspect that they expected in return northern support for their own annexation program. If they were to carry through their designs upon Florida, they must hold New York, Pennsylvania, and Ohio true to the alliance which the Apportionment Bill had shown to be in danger, and Canada was to be the price. That some such bargain was actually made seems clear from events during this session of Congress, but it came only after months of maneuvering.

Grundy of Tennessee had no desire . . . to increase the relative power of the northern states. Nevertheless, he was willing to give a *quid pro quo,* and it was by him that the possibility of a mutually advantageous arrangement was first proclaimed in Congress. "The idea I am about to advance," he declared in the House, December 9, "is at war, I know,

with the sentiments of the gentleman from Virginia [Randolph]; I am willing to receive the Canadians as adopted brethren; it will have beneficial political effects; it will preserve the equilibrium of the Government. When Louisiana shall be fully peopled, the Northern States will lose their power; they will be at the discretion of others; they can be depressed at pleasure, and then this Union might be endangered — I therefore feel anxious not only to add the Floridas to the South, but the Canadas to the North of this empire."

The offer of a bargain was sufficiently plain, and it was probably in reply to it that John A. Harper of New Hampshire, one of the most insistent of the northern expansionists, announced three weeks later his belief that "the Author of Nature has marked our limits in the south, by the Gulf of Mexico; and in the north, by the regions of eternal frost."

Grundy and Harper thus seemed to be in entire agreement, and it is possible that the two Republican wings might have come to an early understanding had not John Randolph taken it upon himself to warn his southern colleagues of the fraud about to be perpetrated upon them, and incidentally to drag the sectional issue into full daylight.

"He could but smile," Randolph declared, December 10, "at the liberality of the gentleman [Grundy] in giving Canada to New York, in order to strengthen the Northern balance of power, while at the same time he forewarned her that the Western scale must preponderate. Mr. R[andolph] said he could almost fancy that he saw the Capitol in motion towards the falls of the Ohio — after a short sojourn taking its flight to the Mississippi, and finally alighting in Darien; which, when the gentleman's dreams are realized, will be a most eligible seat of government for the new Republic (or Empire) of the two Americas! ... He was unwilling, however, under present circumstances, to take Canada at the risk of the Constitution — to embark in a common cause with France and be dragged at the heels of the car of some Burr or Bonaparte. For a gentleman from Tennessee or Genesee, or Lake Champlain, there may be some prospect of advantage. Their hemp will bear a great price by the exclusion of foreign supply. In that too the great importers were deeply interested. The upper country on the Hudson and the Lakes would be enriched by the supplies for the troops, which they alone could furnish. They would have the exclusive market; to say nothing of the increased preponderance from the acquisition of Canada and that section of the Union [sic], which the Southern and Western States had already felt so severely in the apportionment bill."

Mr. Randolph then turned to the defenceless state of the Chesapeake and the danger which, with the militia drawn off to Canada, might arise from the negro population, corrupted, so he declared, by the French Revolution.

Six days later Randolph renewed his attack:

"Sir, if you go to war it will not be for the protection of, or defence of your maritime rights. Gentlemen from the north have been taken up into some high mountain and shown all the kingdoms of the earth; and Canada seems tempting in their sight. That rich vein of Genesee land, which is said to be even better on the other side of the lake than on this. Agrarian cupidity, not maritime right, urges the war. Ever since the report of the Committee on Foreign Relations came into the House, we have heard but

one word — like the whippoor-will, but one eternal monotonous tone — Canada! Canada! Canada! Not a syllable about Halifax, which unquestionably should be our great object in a war for martime security. It is to acquire a preponderating northern influence, that you are to launch into war...."

[Randolph apparently expressed a sentiment rather common among southern congressmen. In February, their votes defeated a proposal to establish a provisional army of 20,000 men, tailored to the requirements of a campaign against Canada. The sectional bargain appeared to be in jeopardy.]

More than two months later southern Republicans remained in the same doubtful position toward the conquest of Canada — at least if we may believe a bit of cautious testimony from one of the more moderate Federalists, Senator Bayard of Delaware.

"Judging from the course of conversation," wrote Bayard in May, "it would seem that the plan of the war is changing. The Western and Southern Gentlemen are alarmed at a point very seriously insisted upon by the Northern — that in case Canada is conquered it shall be divided into states and inalienably incorporated into the Union. You will see the great and permanent weight which such an event would throw into the northern scale. No proposition could have been more frightful to the southern men, and it seems that they had never thought of what they were to do with Canada before, in case they conquered the country, but they prefer that Canada should remain a British Province rather than become States of America. The consequence has been that they now begin to talk of maritime war, and of the ocean being the only place where G[reat] Britain is tangible. What I am now telling you is not an affair generally or publicly spoken of. It has existed but a short time and passes as yet in whispers and a semi-confidential way. I am inclined to think it true and likely to produce important results."

The most active man in pressing the point mentioned by Bayard — that Canada if conquered must be retained — was John A. Harper of New Hampshire. Less than two weeks after the date of Bayard's letter, Harper wrote to the New Hampshire executive a forecast of the opening moves of the war. Among them, he thought, would be "an address to the people of Canada that they shall be protected in their persons, property and religion, and that that country shall be incorporated with and become a part of the Union. Upon the last proposition," Harper continued, "I have had much labor. I have no idea of having a war for several years to conquer the British Provinces and then surrender them by negotiation and unless we can have a pledge that once conquered, they shall be retained, I will never give my vote to send an army there. I have reflected much upon this question and used all my influence to have it effected. I am in hopes of being successful. Until I made the proposition I believe it was not agitated by any member of Congress or of the Executive."

Harper's letter supplies the key to Bayard's. Harper was pressing for a pledge that Canada should be retained. The southern members were reluctant — "I have had much labor," said Harper. We may piece out the story with some expressions in a speech of Senator Hunter of Rhode Island in the following winter. "The declaration that Canada should be conquered and retained," according to Hunter's story, "was the exacted pledge

of the Northern men who voted for the war." The wording is noticeably similar to Harper's and indicates that Harper secured his object. But Senator Hunter also related how it was managed. The terms of the bargain, he declared, were "an enlargement and arrondissement of the territory at the two extremities: a fair division of the spoil," and he added that the southern men had taken the position: "We consent that you may conquer Canada, permit us to conquer Florida."

Senator Hunter was a Federalist, and his testimony relative to Republican logrolling is to be received with caution, but this statement fits so neatly with the known situation that we cannot disregard it.

That such a bargain as he described had been reached is further indicated by events in Congress immediately following the declaration of war. War was declared June 18. Next day Troup of Georgia moved a resolution in the House instructing the committee formerly appointed to consider relations with the Spanish-American colonies, to inquire into the expediency of authorizing the President to occupy East and West Florida, and to report to the House on that subject. June 22, Mitchill of New York, chairman of the committee, introduced a bill which was intended eventually to embody the agreement between the two expansionist groups. The bill as introduced concerned only Florida. It authorized the President "to occupy and hold, the whole or any part of East Florida, including Amelia Island, and also those parts of West Florida which are not now in possession and under the jurisdiction of the United States." An appropriation of $100,000 was provided, and the President was authorized to use the military and naval forces to effect the occupation, and to set up a temporary government in the territory occupied. Finally, to palliate the character of the seizure, it was provided, "That the section of country herein designated, that is situated to the Eastward of the river Perdido, may be the subject of further negotiation." The bill was promptly passed by the House, June 25, and sent to the Senate.

. . . Senator Crawford of Georgia was in close touch, and also in close sympathy, with the measures by which parts of East Florida had already been occupied by American troops. It is not unlikely that Harper should have gone to him in his efforts to secure support for the annexation of Canada. Crawford, at any rate, now came forward with an amendment to the House bill which coupled Canada with Florida, carefully balancing point with point. Crawford's amendment, which the Senate adopted July 2, provided that, if the United States should obtain possession "of the British provinces in North America, or either of them," the President should have authority to establish therein a temporary government "for the protection and maintenance of the inhabitants of such province or provinces, in the full enjoyment of their property, liberty, and religion." Then, as if to balance the "further negotiation" clause of the Florida provisions, a clause different in form but similar in intent was added: "Provided, That the principles upon which such temporary government shall

be established, shall form no obstacle to the restoration of peace between the two nations."

Under the bill as thus amended the nation stood upon precisely similar footing in its proposed invasions of East Florida and of Canada. Both might be occupied by the nation's armed forces, both might be provided with temporary governments, but in the case of each, the question of permanent possession was left open to further negotiation. The amendment was accepted by both wings of the war party; every Republican who had voted for the declaration of war supported it, except Smith of Maryland. The bill was passed to third reading next day. Then, when the passage of the bill — and with it the sealing of the compact between North and South — seemed assured, three of the foes of the administration — Giles, Leib, and Pope — swung over to join the Federalists. With them voted the two New York senators, Gilman of New Hampshire, and Smith of Maryland — men whom the previous votes on the bill had already shown in opposition. The votes of any two of them would have passed the measure; without them it was defeated by a vote of 14 to 16.

Thus, when northern and southern expansionists had patched up their differences, Republican factionalism, with its center in Pennsylvania, Maryland, and Virginia, put the whole annexation program in jeopardy. [But this came only after war had been declared.]

The next major interpretation of Western war sentiment was put forward by GEORGE R. TAYLOR half a dozen years after Pratt's book. Like several other authors quoted in this volume, Taylor is essentially a historian of the American economy, and his best known work, *The Transportation Revolution*, describes American economic growth after 1815. The essay reprinted below reflects his interest in this side of the nation's history.*

Depression Stirs Western War Spirit

Agrarian discontent has so often played an important part in our history that it is surprising that its importance in the Mississippi Valley preceding the War of 1812 has not been recognized. Western agriculture suffered, as this paper will show, a severe economic depression in the years just before the war, and this depression was an important factor in determining the support which the frontier gave first to the Embargo and Non-intercourse acts and finally to war. To understand western discontent, something of the situation in earlier years must be known. The examination of western economic conditions may well begin, therefore, with the period of prosperity which preceded the hard times of 1808-12.

In the first decade of the nineteenth century, the hunting and trapping frontier receded to the west and north, and, over wide areas, the valleys of the Ohio and lower Mississippi became definitely a farming country. For several years following the Louisiana Purchase this new agricultural West experienced a pronounced boom. The usual optimism and exaggerated anticipations of wealth which we have since learned to expect in such periods were abundantly present. The depression which accompanied the Peace of Amiens had been largely attributed by western farmers to Spanish interference with the Mississippi trade at New Orleans. When, therefore, news reached the West that the United States

*Reprinted from "Agrarian Discontent in the Mississippi Valley Preceding the War of 1812" by George R. Taylor, *Journal of Political Economy*, vol. XXXIX (1931), pp. 471-474, 484-485, 487-494, 497, 499-505, by permission of The University of Chicago Press.

had purchased Louisiana, the frontiersmen believed that serious obstacles to western prosperity were a thing of the past.

Everywhere on the frontier people now believed that they saw the dawn of a new and prosperous day. A Kentucky editor declared that the undisturbed right to navigate the Mississippi insured in itself "...a perpetual union of the states, and lasting prosperity to the Western country." And a contributor to the *Scioto Gazette* wrote: "...No ruinous fluctuations in commerce need now be apprehended. Agriculture may depend upon those steady markets which trade shall open to industry."

With this spirit abroad it is not surprising that settlers came crowding to the frontier in unprecedented numbers. Soon after the transfer of Louisiana to the United States, a great influx of pioneer farmers and adventurers began into the area bounded by New Orleans on the south and the frontier settlements in central Ohio on the north, and reached its crest in the boom years of 1805 and 1806....

A wave of optimism once started by a propitious event — in this case the removal of Spanish control over Mississippi River trade — may, as subsequent crazes and booms have shown, go far on its own momentum. Moreover, the ambitious hopes of the frontier farmers had some solid basis. Good land was cheap; and, the land once cleared, crops flourished and harvests were abundant. What could be more encouraging to the farmers who had just left exhausted soils on the eastern coast or the infertile lands of the Appalachian Plateau? ...

From the vantage point of over one hundred years after the event, the fact is clear enough that the western agriculturist of 1805 was, despite elimination of Spanish interference on the Mississippi, abundant harvests, increased immigration, and high prices for western products, much more sanguine in his expectations of prosperity than fundamental conditions justified. Even without the embargo and non-intercourse of 1808 and 1809, it cannot be doubted that the bubble of 1805 would soon have burst. Time, it is true, was to iron out many of the obstacles to western prosperity; in the long run the West was in truth a land of promise. But underlying weaknesses existed in the immediate situation. . . . [Among these were difficulties of transportation by land and river; underdeveloped financial machinery, particularly a shortage of banks; and only rudimentary marketing organizations.]

No one of the drawbacks ... nor all of them together were necessarily fatal to western hopes, for, though difficulties are great and costs high, if prices are still higher, prosperity may yet be obtained. Still these difficulties surely tended to make the West of this period a sort of marginal area in relation to world-markets. When world-prices ruled high, Monongahela and Kentucky flour could be disposed of in competition with that from Virginia and Maryland. Likewise, when cotton and tobacco brought good prices, the Kentucky and Tennessee product could be sold along with that of the Atlantic states and still yield a profit to distant western farmers. But when markets were dull and prices falling, western producers not only saw the fading of their roseate hopes but often enough found themselves in desperate straits to secure necessary imported commodities or to meet obligations for land bought on credit when hopes ran high with prices.

Free navigation of the Mississippi, unprecedented immigration, and unusually high prices had brought a great wave of optimism to the West following 1803, despite the underlying difficulties just considered. The peak year proved to be 1805, but times were relatively good in 1806 and 1807 except for those parts of the West which were adversely affected by glutted markets and lower prices for west-country provisions. Acute depression did not come until 1808. The price situation of that year speaks for itself. Since 1805 the index of wholesale prices of western products at New Orleans had fallen over 20 per cent. Except for hemp growers in Kentucky and infant manufacturing interests at Pittsburgh and Lexington, practically the whole West was prostrated....

Our attention in this paper is centered primarily upon western attempts to mend their failing fortunes through supporting commercial coercion and war. An understanding of the course of frontier opinion in respect to these measures involves, first, a realization of the degree of support which the West gave to the Embargo Act of December, 1807, and, second, an appreciation of the importance of economic motives in prompting the West to support a measure accompanied, as this one was, by widespread depression. An examination of the situation reveals that in his policy of commercial coercion President Jefferson received no more faithful support than that which came from western congressmen. Almost to a man, they voted for the original act of December, 1807, which placed a general embargo on foreign trade; and they supported him loyally in the numerous measures which followed to make its operation effective. When, in November, 1808, the House of Representatives by the very close count of fifty-six to fifty-eight voted to continue the measure in effect, the western members were solidly with the majority. And the next spring, when others weakened, western congressmen stood out for the continuance of the embargo, or, failing that, for the adoption of a non-intercourse act. A westerner, George W. Campbell, of Tennessee, was one of the Senate leaders who held out most firmly against any loosening of commercial restrictions.

... [T]he frontier was, as a whole, no less favorable to the embargo than its representatives in Congress. The commercial boycott had been successfully used against England in our earlier struggles, and it now seemed to westerners a natural and powerful weapon. State legislatures, local political leaders, and public meetings expressed their enthusiastic approval. Most western newspapers printed articles which ardently championed the embargo. Opinion was so united in its favor in Tennessee as to call forth the following statement: "We never witnessed a greater unanimity to prevail in any considerable district of country, and relative to any important question, than now prevails throughout the state of Tennessee respecting the measures of the General Government. The voice of approbation is universal." Two months after the measure had been superseded by the Non-Intercourse Act, they were still drinking toasts to it in Vincennes. Perhaps at that distant frontier outpost they had not yet learned of its repeal....

The western farmer was quite willing to admit his lack of interest in the carrying trade. Even impressment of seamen, though to be deplored, did not seem to him very important. But he did want adequate markets and good prices for his produce, and these he believed impossible so long as Great Britain restricted the West Indian market, forbade direct trade with the Continent, and placed exceedingly burdensome duties upon American imports into Great Britain. In the eyes of the western farmer, the depression of 1808 was primarily the result of the belligerents' decrees and orders in council, not of the embargo which he regarded as a highly desirable act, designed as a measure of retaliation to force the abandonment by foreign nations of their destructive interference with the marketing of our surplus products. "Who now blames the embargo?" demanded a Cincinnati editor. "Who considers it a matter of French interest or procurement? Who does not allow it to be a *saving measure?* ... The embargo was produced by the foreign belligerent powers. They made it wise, just and necessary. They made its continuance necessary."

In Congress western representatives made no effort to conceal their economic interest in the embargo. Said Senator Pope of Kentucky, in stating the very core of the argument in defense of this measure:

What, Mr. President, is our situation? ... The dispute between us and the belligerents is not about the carrying trade, but whether we shall be permitted to carry our surplus produce to foreign markets? The privilege of carrying our cotton to market, is one in which, not only the growers themselves are interested, but one which concerns every part of the nation.

He then went on to show that if the embargo were taken off while the orders in council remained in force, cotton would be confined alone to the British market and the price would fall to a ruinously low level. "The necessity," he continued, "... of resisting the British orders and forcing our way to those markets where there is a demand for the article, must be evident to every one who

will consider the subject." In conclusion he added that if England did not change her course war might be necessary.

When the question of continuing the embargo was again debated in the spring of 1809, much was said of markets and prices by those favoring a continuance of restrictive measures. In arguing in the House of Representatives against the proposed repeal of the Embargo Act, George W. Campbell, of Tennessee, declared:

... though you relieve your enemy, you do not furnish any substantial relief to your own people. No, sir, I am convinced that, in less than three months from this day, should this measure succeed, produce will sink below the price which it now bears, or has borne for the last year. There are but few places to which you can go, and those will naturally become glutted for want of competition; and, in a short time, the prices will not pay the original cost. It will, therefore, afford no substantial relief. The relief, too, which it may afford will be partial, confined to certain portions of the Union, and not equally beneficial to the whole. Tobacco will find no market; cotton a temporary market only—for, although Great Britain will receive it, yet, as we have more on hand than she will immediately want, or can make use of, and as we cannot go to France, and our trade to the Continent will undoubtedly be interrupted by Great Britain, she has nothing to do but wait a few days, weeks, or months, and buy it at her own price. ...

By the Non-Intercourse Act, which superseded the Embargo Act in the spring of 1809, direct trade with England and France and their colonies was prohibited. Although there was nothing now to stop an indirect trade with England, the British orders in council still kept American produce from reaching the Continent. On the whole the West did not like the change, and their representatives were right in predicting that such partial opening of trade would glut markets with our products and bring prices still lower. . . .

The course of events during the summer of 1809 was well calculated still further to inflame western hatred for Great Britain and convince the frontier farmers that their surplus could never be exported at a profit until England was somehow forced to permit free trade upon the seas. Prices, although somewhat improved, continued low as compared with pre-embargo years. The Spanish West Indies were now open to American trade; but as, early as June 5, 1809, Havana, the most important Spanish port, was reported surfeited with exportations from New Orleans. Erskine's treaty (April 19, 1809) by which direct trade was to be reopened with England was, at least in some quarters, regarded with suspicion. If it should not result in opening trade with the Continent, it was held that there would be loss for us and gain for England. The editor of the *Lexington Reporter* wrote:

What will be the price of our produce confined and concentrated totally in British warehouses?

Where will be our carrying trade? Why, British merchants and British manufacturers will purchase our productions for the mere expense of shipping and the duties and commissions to London and Liverpool merchants! *Our manufactures will be annihilated.* Britain will have gained a most glorious victory. . . .

What is become of the 100,000 hogsheads of Tobacco exported from the United States?

Will Britain consume and manufacture all our cotton?

No, not one tenth of our Tobacco — not one half of our Cotton; and our flour, our grain, our ashes, our staves, and every other property must center there, and be held as a *pledge for our allegiance.*

In July news reached the West of the extension of the British continental

blockade and of the new duties to be levied upon cotton. The *Reporter*, while bitterly attacking England, held that her insults were the results of our weak policy. "Submission only encourages oppression," wrote the editor, "and Britain will follow up her blow, 'till our chains are fully rivetted." Probably this writer's attitude was extreme. Some westerners were inclined to look with considerable hope upon the Erskine arrangements. But when, in the late summer of 1809, word was carried over the Appalachians that England had repudiated the acts of her minister, the frontier was thoroughly aroused. Public gatherings were called for the denunciation of British perfidy. Editors joined in the clamor, and state legislatures sent communications to the president denouncing England and declaring their willingness to resort to arms.

The editor of the Lexington *Reporter* was not slow to drive home the moral. In a long analysis of the situation he said in part:

The *Farmer* who is complaining of the low price of Cotton, of Tobacco, of any other produce cannot now be deceived of the real cause, he will not attribute it to embargo systems, or to French decrees, for French decrees were in full force when we so anxiously made the experiment of *confining* our trade to Britain, the farmers will see clearly that the orders in council prohibiting and interrupting all commerce to the continent is the only cause for his embarrassments.

. . . The farmer who wishes a market for his produce, must therefore charge his representative in Congress to cast off all temporising. . . .

The winter of 1809–10 found hard times on frontier farms and western sentiment more bitter than ever against the British as the chief cause of the farmers' troubles. The attempt at commercial coercion had failed, but Congress was

not yet ready to declare war. Beginning
May 1, 1810, commerce was freed from
the restrictive measures of our own
government. On the whole, conditions
seemed on the mend in the following
summer, and western farmers were busy
harvesting crops which they hoped might
be floated down the river to good markets in 1811. Some thought they perceived a promise of better times, while
others saw no assurance of prosperity
until foreign restrictions should be withdrawn.

But, instead of improving, conditions
actually grew seriously worse during the
next two years. Wholesale prices of
western products were below even those
of 1808 in the year before the war. . . .
[While the Ohio River area was seriously
hit by this depression, the tobacco, hemp,
and cotton growers suffered most, since
the prices of these commodities fell dis-
astrously.]

Increased bitterness toward Great Britain and a renewed determination to force
her to repeal her commercial restrictions
accompanied the depression of 1811–12.
But frontiersmen showed no desire to
repeat the attempt at commercial coercion; past failures had shaken their faith
in pacific measures. The new attitude is
epitomized in the following toast offered
at a Fourth of July celebration held at
Frankfort in 1811: "Embargoes, non-
intercourse, and negotiations, are but illy
calculated to secure our rights. . . . Let us
now try old Roman policy, and maintain
them with the sword. . . ."

To one familiar with the situation on
the frontier in 1808–10 it can hardly
come as a surprise that, in the same
breath in which the farmers deplored
their ruined agriculture, they urged war
against England. Both on the frontier
and in the halls of Congress westerners

now demanded war as a necessary measure for economic relief.

When word of President Madison's
warlike message to the Twelfth Congress
reached western Pennsylvania, the editor
of the Pittsburgh *Mercury* declared himself attached to peace but if necessary
ready to fight for commerce. And at the
other end of the frontier, Governor
W. C. C. Claiborne, in his inaugural
address before the Louisiana state legislature, declared: "The wrongs of England have been long and seriously felt;
they are visible in the decline of our sea
towns, in the ruin of our commerce and
the languor of agriculture." Perhaps the
statements of the somewhat bombastic
governor must not be taken too seriously.
But the following by a Louisiana cotton
planter seems to come directly, if not
from the heart, at least from the pocket-
book:

Upon the subject of cotton we are not such
fools, but we know that there is not competition in the European market for that article, and that the British are giving us what
they please for it — and, if we are compelled
to give it away, it matters not to us, who
receives it. But we happen to know that we
should get a much greater price for it, for
we have some idea of the extent of the Continent, and the demand there for it; and we
also know that the British navy is not so
terrible as you would make us believe; and,
therefore, upon the score of lucre, as well as
national honor, we are ready.

In Kentucky even the editor of the
lone Federalist paper the *American Republic* denounced foreign restrictions as
the cause for the depressed prices for
western produce. He differed from the
Democrats only in that he blamed not
England but France, and also, of course,
the Democratic administration for the
hard times. But this editor had almost

no popular following. His paper, which went out of existence in the spring of 1812, represented little more than his own personal opinions.

When aggressive action toward England seemed imminent late in 1811, the [Lexington, Ky.] *Reporter,* which had advocated war to secure markets as early as 1809, printed an editorial saying: "It appears likely that our government will at last make war, to produce a market for our Tobacco, Flour and Cotton." And as Congress hesitated over the fatal step, the *Reporter* continued to clamor for war. In April a communication printed in that paper violently attacked England as the source of western difficulties and declared that western hemp raisers would be completely ruined by English measures. And the editor himself wrote in similar vein:

We are . . . aware that many circumstances combined to reduce the price of produce. The *British Orders in Council,* which still prevent the exportation of cotton, tobacco, &c. to the continent of Europe, *are the chief* — (at the same time confining every thing to their own glutted market) whilst those continue, the carrying trade will be very limited, and bear down considerably the consumption and price of hemp, yarns, &c.

In what was perhaps the most curious and at the same time most revealing article to appear in the West, this same editor wrote:

Should those *quid* representatives and *quid* members of the administration support war measures after Britain has forced us into war, they support it only for *popularity,* and fear of *public* opinion. Not that their hearts are with their country—But with the British agents and U. States aristocracy.—But the scalping knife and tomahawk of *British savages, is now, again devastating our frontiers.*
Hemp at three dollars.

Cotton at twelve dollars.
Tobacco at nine shillings.

Thus will our farmers, and wives and children, continue to be *ruined* and *murdered,* whilst those half-way, *quid,* execrable measures and delays preponderate.

Either *federal* or democratical energy would preserve us all.

When it is remembered that the streets of Lexington were safely distant from the nearest conceivable point of Indian depredation, the editor's reference to economic ruin and the depressed price of commodities appears somehow more sincere than his dramatic reference to danger of tomahawk and scalping knife.

Nor did the economic aspect of the situation fail to find emphasis in the debates at Washington. In the discussions there on declaring war, western congressmen repeatedly emphasized the economic argument. Said Felix Grundy, of Tennessee, a leader of the western War Hawks second only to Henry Clay: ". . . inquire of the Western people why their crops are not equal to what they were in former years, they will answer that industry has no stimulus left, since their surplus products have no markets." And Samuel McKee, of Kentucky, expressed frontier exasperation with those who counseled delay, in the following words:

How long shall we live at this poor dying rate, before this non-importation law will effect the repeal of the Orders in Council? Will it be two years or twenty years? The answer is in the bosom of futurity. But, in the meantime, our prosperity is gone; our resources are wasting; and the present state of things is sapping the foundations of our political institutions by the demoralization of the people.

So much has been made of the youthful enthusiasm of the War Hawks, of their national feeling and keen resentment of foreign insults, that it may possibly appear to some that these western leaders were great hypocrites who talked of national honor but acted secretly from economic motives. By way of extenuation it may be suggested that national honor and national interest seldom fail to coincide. Furthermore, the western leaders made no secret of their "interests" even though they did have much to say of "honor." Clay demanded vigorous measures against England, declaring that through failure to fight we lost both commerce and character. "If pecuniary considerations alone are to govern," he said, "there is sufficient motive for the war." Three months later, when writing to the editor of the *Kentucky Gazette* assuring him that war would yet be declared, Clay did not hesitate to state in a letter which was probably intended for publication: "In the event of war, I am inclined to think that article [hemp] will command a better price than it now does."

Confusion has sometimes arisen from the failure to realize that commercial privileges were as essential to those who produced goods for foreign exportation as for the merchants who gained by performing the middleman service. John Randolph did accuse the Democratic majority in Congress of being the dupes of eastern merchants. But one has only to read the words of the southern and western advocates of war to find that their position was clear and straightforward enough. Said Felix Grundy:

It is not the carrying trade, properly so called, about which this nation and Great Britain are at present contending. Were this the only question now under consideration, I should feel great unwillingness . . . to involve the nation in war, for the assertion of a right, in the enjoyment of which

the community at large are not more deeply concerned. The true question in controversy, is of a very different character; it involves the interest of the whole nation. It is the right of exporting the productions of our own soil and industry to foreign markets.

Repeatedly this matter came up, and as often western representatives clearly stated their position. Henry Clay left the speaker's chair to explain:

We were but yesterday contending for the indirect trade — the right to export to Europe the coffee and sugar of the West Indies. Today we are asserting our claim to the direct trade — the right to export our cotton, tobacco, and other domestic produce to market.

Too much has been made of Randolph's charge against the War Hawks that they sought the conquest of Canada, and not enough of his declarations that western representatives were much influenced by consideration of their own advantage. It is true that pro-war Democrats of the coast states hurried to deny that their western colleagues were actuated by "selfish motives." But Calhoun's reply to Randolph is worth quoting, for, although apparently intended as a denial, it is actually an admission of the charge. He is reported as saying:

. . . the gentleman from Virginia attributes preparation for war to everything but its true cause. He endeavored to find it in the probable rise of the price of hemp. He represents the people of the Western States as willing to plunge our country into war for such base and precarious motives. I will not reason on this point. I see the cause of their ardor, not in such base motives, but in their known patriotism and disinterestedness. No less mercenary is the reason which he attributes to the Southern States. He says, that the non-importation act has reduced cotton to nothing, which has produced feverish impatience. Sir, I acknowledge the cotton of our farms is worth but little; but not for the cause assigned by the gentleman from Virginia. The people of that section do not reason as he does; they do not attribute it to the efforts of their Government to maintain peace and independence of their country; they see in the low price of the produce, the hand of foreign injustice; they know well, without the market to the Continent, the deep and steady current of supply will glut that of Great Britain; they are not prepared for the colonial state to which again that Power is endeavoring to reduce us.

Not only were westerners accused of seeking war for their own economic advantage, but many held they were mistaken in believing that war with England would bring them the results they sought. Federalists and anti-war Democrats repeatedly declared in Congress that war would not open markets or restore the price of hemp, tobacco, or cotton. These speeches, cogent as they often were, failed in their purpose of dissuading the frontiersmen from demanding war, but they are convincing evidence to us that the anti-war minority, no less than the majority which favored the conflict, recognized clearly enough the important relation of economic motives to the war spirit.

As noted at the outset, factors other than those emphasized in this study undoubtedly played a part in bringing on the war. The expansionist sentiment, which Professor Julius W. Pratt has emphasized, was surely present. English incitement to Indian depredations and Spanish interference with American trade through Florida should be noted, as should also the fact that the frontiersmen sought every possible pretext to seize the coveted Indian lands. Restrictions on the carrying trade, even impressment of seamen, may have had some effect in influencing western opinion. No doubt the traditional hostility of the Republican party toward England played a part. Many veterans of the Revolutionary War had settled upon western lands, and time had not failed to magnify the glory of their achievements or to add to the aggressive ardor of their patriotism.

But important as these factors may have been, the attitude of the western settler can hardly be evaluated without an understanding of his economic position. He was, after all, typically an ambitious farmer who moved to the Mississippi Valley in order to make a better living. In the boom times following the Louisiana Purchase he had regarded the western frontier as a veritable promised land. Moreover, the fertile river valleys rewarded his toil with luxuriant harvests. But somehow prosperity eluded him. When, in spite of tremendous difficulties, he brought his produce to market, prices were often so low as to make his venture a failure.

We know now that the farmers' troubles were, in no small degree, fundamentally matters of transportation, of communication, and of imperfect marketing and financial organization. But is it unexpected that in their disappointment (and not unlike their descendants of today who still are inclined to magnify political factors) they put the blame for their economic ills upon foreign restriction of their markets and supported the Embargo and Non-Intercourse acts as weapons to coerce the European belligerents to give them what they regarded as their rights? And when peaceful methods failed and prices fell to even lower levels, is it surprising that the hopeful settlers of earlier years became the War Hawks of 1812?

MARGARET K. LATIMER has applied the Taylor thesis to South Carolina. The appearance of her results in 1956 marked the end of a twenty-five year period during which, despite Burt's able summary, no new interpretations of the causes of the war had been put forward. Moreover, here sharing Burt's view, the author suggests that it was not only Western bellicosity that needed to be explained if one were to understand the coming of the War of 1812. With some modifications, Mrs. Latimer's thesis could be applied to other non-Western but agricultural areas. Although South Carolina produced several leading war hawks, among them John C. Calhoun, Langdon Cheves, and William Lowndes, other seaboard states also sent men with prowar sentiments to Congress.*

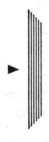

The South Also Feels the Depression

South Carolina's agrarian economy was one of the major factors which drew her originally into the Republican fold. But it was the growing preoccupation of South Carolina with the international commerce necessary to make agriculture profitable that took her somewhat off the path envisaged by Jefferson. Attacking the traditional Jeffersonian international policy, the Republican William Lowndes said to Congress, "The interests of agriculture and commerce are inseparable.

What is commerce but the exchange of the surplus produce of . . . one nation for those of another? . . . it is this commerce which makes agriculture valuable." Such a positive stand was not unusual, for South Carolina never demonstrated a very close adherence to the national party. The local Republican group so well represented the interests of the planting-business community of the state as a whole that its standard-bearers received almost no opposition from the

*Margaret K. Latimer, "South Carolina — A Protagonist of the War of 1812," *American Historical Review*, vol. LXI (1955-1956), pp. 921-929. Reprinted with the permission of the *American Historical Review*.

Federalists in elections for national representatives, and the delegates in turn exercised a notable independence and lack of partisanship in Congress. Edward Hooker's description of Wade Hampton, one of the prosperous upcountry Republicans, was almost generally applicable to South Carolinians: "In his politics he is, I hardly know what. He is called a republican; yet he certainly has many notions and sentiments which are more characteristic of federalism. And he does not hesitate to condemn openly, and unequivocably some measures of the republican party."

Calhoun, Cheves, and Lowndes had come to prominence in this era of independent Republicanism and conservative political unanimity. Calhoun was from Scotch-Irish upcountry stock, although the holdings of his father put him easily in the category of "planter." After early training at the academy of Moses Waddell in Georgia, Calhoun went to Yale, where his seriousness and sternness must have made him well fitted for Timothy Dwight's domain. This Federalist president had a prevading influence over the students at Yale College, and it seems unlikely that Calhoun was untouched by his ideas. Experience in the Charleston law office of Henry W. DeSaussure and formal study at Litchfield Law School in Connecticut under Federalists James Gould and Tapping Reeve contributed further to Calhoun's background of conservatism. In 1811, his marriage to Floride Calhoun, a cousin who belonged to wealthy Charlestonian society, gave the Republican uplander a direct tie to the older, more staid South Carolina lowcountry.

Calhoun was a lawyer in the Piedmont region at the time that the Chesapeake-Leopard affair provoked indignant public meetings in many localities. His first chance at public oratory came when he was requested by the Abbeville committee to write and present its resolutions denouncing the incident; shortly thereafter he was elected to the state legislature, and in 1810 he became a representative to the United States Congress.

Langdon Cheves, also newly elected to Congress in 1810, had both upcountry and lowcountry connections as did Calhoun. He was born in Abbeville, a Piedmont district, and later became a lawyer in Charleston. The third new congressman, William Lowndes, was of lowcountry planting origin, and his attractive and intelligent wife was a confirmed Federalist, the daughter of Thomas Pinckney.

Calhoun, Cheves, and Lowndes, Republicans with backgrounds strongly marked by conservative influences, expressed in the Twelfth Congress the conservatism which had become characteristic of South Carolina's "Federal"-Republicanism. All three were men of outstanding leadership abilities; and, when they made demands in the interest of their state, they also revealed a strong bent toward nationalization. Though nationalism can be the manifestation of both liberal and conservative movements, in 1811 nationalizing measures were definitely the latter. The conservatives during the Constitution-making era were the nationalists, and the South Carolinians were of this breed — conservatives in their desire to preserve the prevailing socioeconomic system of their state. They sought federal power to protect this way of life. Their nationalism was thus, in a sense, a sectionalism in disguise.

Calhoun, Cheves, and Lowndes were elected to Congress in 1810 with "reference to the critical condition of the country." They were all in a belligerent mood, and they had spoken vigorously in pre-election campaigns. A clear statement of Calhoun's views on international affairs had been set forward as early as the Republican caucus in 1808: reviewing the struggle between the United States and European powers, he labeled the resort to the restrictive system an inefficient means of preserving American rights and pointed out that war with England was unavoidable. He later saw "in the low price of the produce, the hand of foreign injustice." British minister Augustus J. Foster, who met the representatives in Washington, noted that the South Carolina members of Congress were "resolute," "particularly the younger Deputies...who seemed to have great influence and were very cool and decided on the propriety of going to war in order to protect the Commerce of the Country." The South Carolina congressmen had a vital interest in the "Commerce of the Country," because on it depended the future of the prosperous economic developments which had taken place in South Carolina during the first decade of the nineteenth century.

By 1811 the entire state was in the middle of a tremendous cotton boom. The value and practicability of upland-grown short-staple cotton had become immediately apparent upon invention of the cotton gin and were demonstrated after the introduction of the gin into South Carolina in 1801; at the same time the demand for cotton went up as machine methods of manufacture became standard in England. When the slave trade was reopened in 1803, cotton production proceeded at full speed. South Carolina doubled its cotton output in the ten years following 1801, producing forty million pounds in 1811; the state had begun to export approximately forty per cent of the total cotton exports of the United States. As David Ramsay wrote in 1808, cotton "has trebled the price of

land suitable to its growth, and when the crop succeeds and the market is favorable, the annual income of those who plant it is double to what it was before the introduction of cotton."

The increased use of the Negro slave was of course necessary for the phenomenal expansion of upland cotton, and during these years a constantly growing number of farmers and planters acquired property in slaves. It is important to note, however, that in twenty-three out of twenty-eight districts in 1810 whites still outnumbered blacks, the popular image depicting masses of Negroes working on all the farm lands being far from correct. True, in coast districts such as Charleston and Colleton the black population was actually much greater than the white, but here cotton and rice production had probably been expanded to the limit before 1800 since the percentage of slave population even decreased slightly in the period 1800–1810. It was the upcountry legislators who insisted on the reopening of the slave trade in 1803, for it was their region in which cotton and slavery were spreading. A look at the United States Census figures for 1790, 1800, and 1810 shows as expected a steady increase in slaves for upcountry districts, the largest proportional gain coming after 1800....

When the upland area like the coast became a significant producer of cotton, South Carolina could boast an amazing unity of economic interest. Corollary to this economic development was of course the spread of political power into the upcountry and the resulting era in which political and cultural oneness increased steadily. This unanimity of interest, political and economic, exhibited itself under the name of Republicanism.

The enactment of the embargo by the federal government in 1808 exactly coincided with the full realizations of South Carolinians that the primary economic interests of the state were much the same from coast to hill country, that a continuance of the cotton-planting system was essential to all areas. The discomforts brought on by the embargo gave the state an even greater unity as both sections were prey to the economic forces which made prices go up at the same time that profits decreased. The southern agriculturalists incurred constant expenses whether or not their products sold, but the traditional planting system had to be kept. Manufacturing had no chance to develop because after 1803 the capital of the South had gone into buying slaves; the area was already in debt to New England.

The Charleston *Courier* reported on January 20, 1808, that cotton was down to twenty-five cents per pound, and on February 10, 1810, that it had fallen to fourteen cents. A contemporary observer reported that in order to make ends meet, the South Carolinians had to get at least twenty cents for their cotton. One should note that the critical drop in price came between 1808 and 1810; this difference may partially account for South Carolina's growing concern with the world situation during that period, for attitudes which varied from passive endurance to active belligerence. The South Carolina legislature in June, 1808, had expressed its willingness to enforce the embargo, but in reporting the resolutions to Jefferson, Speaker Joseph Alston did tell the President that they represented a wholehearted patriotism, not necessarily a "perfect unanimity of political opinion." As economic conditions became tighter, there was growing resistance to the embargo and to its successor, nonintercourse.

Calhoun's public speech against the embargo in 1808 has already been cited. Governor Charles Pinckney in December, 1807, blamed disputes with Great Britain for "an almost total stagnation of commerce and stoppage of the sale of produce"; this caused "the great inconvenience of merchants and planters." Fear that the international situation would bring the loss of markets gave impetus to such news stories as that which noted the phenomenal growth of South American cotton sales in Liverpool. By June, 1812, there were reports that cotton planters had been forced to turn to corn, that some upcountry men were turning to wheat. The situation in Charleston is well mirrored in the letters of Margaret Izard Manigault to her mother: cotton prices of 1811 were down to eight cents; money in town was almost nonexistent; and worst of all, since early 1809 there had scarcely been a party.

South Carolina depended on unrestricted trade — on "commerce" as British minister Foster called it — because this was a region where people cultivated the soil, sold most of what they produced, and purchased most of what they consumed. Although the nonimportation law which succeeded the embargo in 1809 was often unenforced, general economic conditions kept on the downgrade as long as there was a controversy with England, the chief purchaser and provider in the South. By the time of the Twelfth Congress, the tone of the South Carolina legislature had changed notably from that of 1808. This group sent resolutions to President Madison demanding that definite action be taken to protect commerce and the honor of the nation. A firm stand from the beginning, it was explained, might have prevented much loss to agriculture. D. R. Williams vigorously expressed the sentiments of his state before Congress:

But what is the condition of the commerce with Great Britain.... Truly miserable.... How is tobacco affected?... Inquire into the state of the cotton market; where is the crop of 1810? A curse to him who meddled with it. Where is that of 1811? Rotting at home in the hands of the grower, waiting the repeal of the Orders in Council.

South Carolina had developed a decided urge for war. Excited by considerations of her primary livelihood, the export trade in cotton, South Carolina became one of the main protagonists of the conflict. This was not the largest or wealthiest state in the union, but it had one special qualification for national leadership in 1812 — the most at stake in the domestic export trade; South Carolina had more exports per individual white person than any other state in the union. With only 3.6 per cent of the total white population of the United States, South Carolina exported 10.3 per cent of the domestic goods. Whether or not fighting a war with England was the logical step to take as a remedy to the commercial and thus agricultural distress is not the question — the South Carolinians of 1812 were convinced that a war would help.

To assess the total internal and external forces which produced the War of 1812 will call for the investigation of a multitude of factors not yet understood. The effort in this paper has been primarily to set forth the position of South Carolina with regard to the war, thereby pointing out in particular the significant part played by the direct trade of the United States, by foreign markets for staple products, in determining the course of events.

In the realm of international diplomacy, A. L. Burt's study goes farther than any other in explaining how the United States, entangled with both Great Britain

and France, finally chose war with Britain. Burt's suggestions regarding the attitudes of the various sections of the United States toward going to war are also well directed. Making note of the fact that the South was sorely pinched for markets (and South Carolina indeed received considerable support in her war effort from Georgia, Virginia, and North Carolina), Burt further points out that the Northeast was "betraying national honor ... for selfish profit." All sources indicate in fact that New England experienced a great shipping and commercial boom because of continuing European hostilities; the United States government went to war to "champion maritime interests ... in spite of their opposition." Burt's observations, apparently sound, are directly supported by the conclusion of this paper that South Carolina, which played a significant role in the congressional campaign for war, had as its primary concern an alleviation of commercial distress.

The thesis of Julius W. Pratt, on the other hand, seems considerably weakened by the findings here reported. The coupling together of the South and Southwest in interpreting the war sentiment is certainly justifiable, but this alliance was not altogether natural, and in many respects the relationships that have been singled out are not the significant ones. Indian troubles may have had some bearing on western sentiment, but these did not pose a serious problem in the South at this date; expansion into Florida was likewise an unimportant urge. The developing political philosophy of Kentucky and Tennessee could rarely be equated with that of conservative cotton producing South Carolina, nor was the latter by 1812 in a position to share the frontier sentiments of the West. Indeed, the support of these states for similar measures in Congress lasted only a few years.

The significant basis of alliance between the South and the Southwest in 1812 was their common cry against foreign depredations on American shipping. As well-explained by G. R. Taylor, when depression replaced the early western prosperity of 1808 and 1809, discontent was rampant and settlers looked madly about them for the causes of their troubles. Economic analysts believe today that these were primarly difficulties within the frontier area itself — matters of transportation, communication, imperfect marketing, and insufficient financial organization. However, the westerners of 1808–1812 grasped for a time at the first likely cause; they began to be painfully aware of foreign restrictions on American commerce, and to these they directed more and more blame for their economic ills. Although western markets were actually far less directly connected to European trade than those of South Carolina, increased demands for western hemp, tobacco, cotton, and flour were hopefully anticipated as results of a war with Great Britain. In 1812, "the right of exporting the productions of our own soil and industry to foreign markets" seemed as real to the hemp and tobacco growers of Kentucky as to the large-scale cotton producers of South Carolina. . . .

In a sense the war marked the end of one era of Jeffersonianism and the beginning of a change in the nature of the Republican party. South Carolina, one of the foremost war-minded leaders, was a state whose Republicanism had never been more than an independent, local movement. The new generation in the Republican party, with an aim to protect and promote the direct commerce of the country that seemed more Federalist than Jeffersonian, was strongly spearheaded by men from the South and the Southwest who worked together successfully in a congressional drive for war. The effective leadership of Henry Clay in the Speaker's chair supplemented by other representatives of the frontier regions must never be minimized, but that provides matter for another paper. Working with Clay, the new delegation from South Carolina was the most aggressive force in Congress.

Paradoxical as it may seem, the desire of South Carolina to preserve and extend the status quo produced a determination not to be undone by the caprices of warring European powers. Going to Congress with the conviction that the older Republican measures would not solve the problems of 1812, South Carolina's young Congressmen Calhoun, Cheves, and Lowndes spoke for the protection of America's foreign commerce and not at all incidentally for the well-being of South Carolina's trade in cotton.

The broadening process begun by Mrs. Latimer was carried a step further by NORMAN K. RISJORD. This scholar, a professor at DePauw University, rejects economic interpretations of the coming of the war as unproved or too narrowly sectional. He seeks out a theme that will explain a rather broad national concurrence, with the possible exception of New England, and finds the answer in a general feeling that British outrages challenged America's honor. Like Taylor, but by a different route, Risjord leads us back to the maritime causes stressed by nineteenth-century historians.*

► *National Honor as the Unifying Force*

The modern tendency to seek material-istic motives and economic factors in all human relations has greatly obscured one of the basic causes of the War of 1812. A generation of historians, brought up on the disillusionment that followed the failure of the attempt to "make the world safe for democracy" in 1919, has persist-ently searched for the hidden economic factors behind all wars. Yet a cursory glance at the statistics of American com-merce in the first decade of the nine-teenth century will show that the War of 1812 was the most uneconomic war the United States has ever fought. A casual search through the letters and speeches of contemporaries reveals that those who fought the war were primarily concerned with the honor and integrity of the nation.

Students of the period are familiar with the standard explanation for the war: the election of 1810, by providing 63 new faces in a House of 142, repre-sented a popular disillusionment with the Jeffersonian system and supplied the new Twelfth Congress with a number of young war hawks, such as Henry Clay, John C. Calhoun, and Felix Grundy, who were determined to assert America's position in the world. Since the loudest demand for strong measures, as well as

*Norman K. Risjord, "1812: Conservatives, War Hawks, and the Nation's Honor," *William & Mary Quarterly*, third series, vol. XVIII (April 1961), pp. 196-210. Reprinted with the permission of the *William & Mary Quarterly* and Norman K. Risjord.

some of the ablest of the war hawks, came from the West, historians have been channeled into a search for reasons why the West should have demanded a war for "free trade and sailors' rights"; the historiography of the period has been almost exclusively concerned with "Western war aims." The desire for land, Canadian or Indian, fear of a British-backed Indian conspiracy, concern over the declining prices of agricultural products and the restriction of markets abroad — all at one time or another have been represented as basic causes of the war.

The weakness in this interpretation is that it virtually ignores the vote on the declaration of war in June 1812. The West may have been influenced by economic as well as patriotic motives, but the West, after all, had only ten votes in the House of Representatives. The South Atlantic states from Maryland to Georgia cast thirty-nine, or nearly half, of the seventy-nine votes for war in 1812. Any explanation of the war must place primary emphasis on the Southern Congressmen, and neither feature of the standard interpretation — the concept of a "revolution" in popular sentiment in 1810 and the emphasis on economic factors — satisfactorily explains their votes for war.

Most of these Southern Congressmen were "old Republicans," conservatives whose political Bible was the Republican platform of 1800 and who had sat in Congress for years. In the South there is no evidence of a sudden popular demand in the election of 1810 for a more energetic government and a more vigorous foreign policy. Maryland, which voted six to three for war in June 1812, had four new members in the Twelfth Congress, one a Federalist. The three new Republicans either won the election

without opposition or they replaced men who had supported military preparations and a stronger foreign policy in the Eleventh Congress.

Virginia, which held her elections for the Twelfth Congress in the spring of 1811, returned a virtually identical delegation of seventeen Republicans and five Federalists. The two Quids, John Randolph and Edwin Gray, were re-elected, as were most of the conservative Republicans of the Eleventh Congress. The Shenandoah Valley remained as solidly Federalist as it had been in 1800, and the tramontane region, the one part of the state that might have been concerned with Indians and Western lands, elected Thomas Wilson, its first Federalist since 1793.

Virginia's election as a whole produced five new Republican members; none apparently was elected on the issue of peace or war. John Wayles Eppes, the only strong leader Virginia had sent to the Eleventh Congress, moved to John Randolph's district in the Southside and was defeated by Randolph in the election. The contest was close even though Eppes never formally declared himself a candidate, but the objections to Randolph centered on his vigorous opposition to the Madison administration. No one maintained that the election of Eppes would ensure stronger measures toward Great Britain. Eppes's seat in his former district was taken by James Pleasants, a war Republican who in the postwar period was to revert to the old Jeffersonian strict constructionist doctrines. In Thomas Jefferson's own district, which included Albemarle County, David S. Garland was replaced by Hugh Nelson, a close friend of James Monroe and member of the "minority" that had supported Monroe against James Madison's election in 1808 because it felt that Madison was too nationalistic. Nelson entered the Twelfth Congress with a decided preference for peace at any price. In the Fredericksburg area the administration regular, Walter Jones, declined to run again, and in the election Major John P. Hungerford defeated John Taliaferro by six votes. Hungerford was a former Quid and had sat on the Monroe electoral committee in 1808. Taliaferro contested the election, received the support of the war hawks in the House, and was awarded the seat. In the Fauquier-Culpeper district John Love, who had generally supported preparedness measures in the Eleventh Congress, declined re-election and was replaced by another war Republican, Dr. Aylet Hawes.

Nearly half the Virginia Congressmen were elected without opposition, and even where there was a contest the election seldom turned on the issue of foreign policy. Typical of Virginia conservatives re-elected in 1811 was John Clopton, who had represented the Richmond district since 1801. If a letter to his constituents published in the *Virginia Argus* is a fair summary of his campaign platform, Clopton was running in support of the non-intercourse law and against the Bank of the United States, giving no indication of any departure from the Jeffersonian system. Clopton had two opponents, one of whom withdrew before the election, while the other made public statements agreeing with Clopton on every issue.

The election of 1810 in North Carolina similarly produced no great change in her representation. Of her twelve Congressmen eight were re-elected, two of them Federalists and one, Richard Stanford, a Randolph Quid. Two of the four newcomers had served in Congress during the Jefferson administration (William Blackledge from 1803 to 1808 and Thomas Blout from 1804 to 1808). The

only new faces in the North Carolina group, Israel Pickens and William R. King, were war hawks, but neither defeated an incumbent.

The political "revolution" in South Carolina in the election of 1810, which produced a unanimous vote for war in June 1812, was more apparent than real. The election of the three great war hawk leaders, John C. Calhoun, William Lowndes, and Langdon Cheves, was more an addition of talent than of numbers to the war party in Congress. In the campaign Calhoun had openly advocated war, but he was elected without opposition since the incumbent — his cousin Joseph Calhoun, a war hawk in the Eleventh Congress — declined re-election and supported him. William Lowndes succeeded to the seat of John Taylor, one of the administration's floor leaders in the Eleventh Congress who had been elected to the Senate. Cheves was elected in 1810 to fill a vacant seat in the Eleventh Congress and was re-elected to the Twelfth.

The other prominent war hawk, David Rogerson Williams, took the seat of his brother-in-law Robert Witherspoon, who declined re-election and threw his support to Williams. Williams, moreover, as a member of the Ninth Congress, had followed John Randolph in rebellion against the Jefferson administration in 1806 and thus fits more into the pattern of the converted conservative. Indeed, as late as May 1812 a Federalist member of the House observed that Williams was still trying to make up his mind between peace and war. The only real contest in South Carolina was the defeat of Lemuel J. Alston by Elias Earle, but no current issue was involved for the two men had taken turns defeating each other for years.

The election in South Carolina illustrates the real significance of the election of 1810. Without any fundamental change in public opinion, and partly by coincidence, South Carolina produced some of the outstanding leaders of the Twelfth Congress. But the change, as in the Western elections that produced Henry Clay and Felix Grundy, was primarily in ability rather than in numbers. Indeed, speaking strictly in terms of numbers, the actual war hawks elected in 1810 were outvoted by Federalists and antiwar Republicans in the Twelfth Congress. The young war hawks from the South and West were certainly able men, and largely by force of character alone they led an unwilling and apathetic country to war.

Yet was leadership alone enough? Several prominent war hawks — Clay, Richard M. Johnson, Ezekiel Bacon, Cheves, and Peter B. Porter — were members of the Eleventh Congress, but despite their ability they had been unable to lead that body in any consistent direction. At least as significant as the suddent appearance of a few talented war hawks in the Twelfth Congress was the gradual conversion of the average Republican from Jeffersonian pacifism to a vigorous defense of America's neutral rights. It was these men, most of them Southerners who had been in Congress for years, who provided the necessary votes for war, just as they had provided the main support for the embargo and nonintercourse laws. Their conversion seems to have stemmed primarily from a disillusionment with the old system of commercial retaliation and a growing realization that the only alternative to war was submission and national disgrace. Every expedient to avoid war honorably had been tried without success. Submission to the orders in council presaged a return to colonial status; war seemed the only alternative. The war, at least as far as the South was concerned, was brought on by men who had had a "bellyful" of England, not by men who were interested in Western lands, or Indians, or prices in the lower Mississippi Valley.

The major weakness in the various economic interpretations is their failure to explain the demand for war in the Middle Atlantic states and in the South. The "expansionists" school of historians, with internal variations, generally maintains that the war was the result of the Western desire for land, in Canada as well as in Indian-dominated Indiana, and that the conquest of Canada was demanded both for its own sake and because the British were backing the Tecumseh confederacy. The difficulty is that the areas most concerned with these problems — Indiana, Illinois, and Michigan — were territories with no vote in Congress. Even Ohio, which presumably had a direct interest in the Wasbash lands, was by no means unanimously in favor of war. Its one representative, Jeremiah Morrow, voted for war in 1812 just as he had voted for the embargo in 1807, but Ohio's two senators, Thomas Worthington and Alexander Campbell, opposed war in 1812 because the nation was unprepared and they feared an Indian attack on the defenseless frontier. Both preferred to retain the old system of commercial retaliation. Some have suggested that Ohio's senators were out of touch with public sentiment, but a recent biographer of Worthington feels that a plebiscite held in the spring of 1812 would probably have shown a majority of the people of Ohio against war. Kentucky and Tennessee, it is true, showed considerable interest in the Indian lands and in Canada, but even so their votes in Congress were hardly enought to carry the country to war.

Julius W. Pratt, leading proponent of

the "expansionist" thesis, circumvented this difficulty by conjecturing a "frontier crescent" of war hawks extending from New Hampshire (John A. Harper) to Kentucky (Clay and Johnson) and Tennessee (Felix Grundy) and ending in South Carolina (Calhoun, Lowndes, and Cheves) and Georgia (George M. Troup). Yet this seems an arbitrary conjunction of dissimilar areas. Why should New Hampshire or Vermont have been interested enough in the Wabash lands to go to war? And how explain a Southern interest in the Wabash or in Canada? Pratt plugged this hole by surmising a bargain between Southern and Western war hawks in which Florida would be brought into the Union to balance the conquest of Canada. The only evidence he cites, however, is one editorial in a Tennessee newspaper.

It is true that Southern war hawks talked much about the conquest of Canada, but they seem to have regarded it as primarily a method of conducting the war rather than as an ultimate objective. Secretary of State Monroe, for instance, felt that Canada might be invaded, "not as an object of the war but as a means to bring it to a satisfactory conclusion." On the other hand there is evidence that some Southerners actually feared the annexation of Canada. John Randolph certainly considered the possibility that Canada might be acquired the best of reasons for not going to war, and a fellow Virginian elected in 1810 wrote home in December 1811: "The New Yorkers and Vermonters are very well inclined to have upper Canada united with them, by way of increasing their influence in the Union." As to the other half of the bargain there is little evidence that outside of the border area the South was much interested in Florida, and recent scholars have tended to minimize the importance

of Florida in the Southern demand for war.

Somewhat more plausible is the economic interpretation of the war in terms of declining farm prices and the restriction of markets abroad. This point of view was first put forth in the early 1930's by George Rogers Taylor, who suggested that the declining price of agricultural products, particularly in the lower Mississippi Valley, may have been a factor in the Western demand for war. The gist of this argument is summed up in a letter of a Louisiana planter of July 25, 1811: "Upon the subject of cotton we are not such fools, but we know that . . . the British are giving us what they please for it. . . . But we happen to know that we should get a much greater price for it, for we have some idea of the extent of the Continent, and the demand there for it; . . . and, therefore, upon the score of lucre, as well as national honor, we are ready." More recently, this argument has been adopted to explain the West-South alliance. Both sections were concerned with the declining prices of the great staple exports, cotton, tobacco, and hemp, and were inclined to blame the British orders in council for restricting their markets. The South and West, in this view, went to war primarily to defend the right to export their products without interference from Britain.

That prices for these great staples declined gradually throughout the first decade of the century cannot be denied, but to what extent the British blockades were responsible is more difficult to determine. The direct trade in agricultural products was not generally affected by the orders in council; not till the winter of 1811-12 did the British interfere with cotton shipments, though their action at that time helped to justify war — at least in the mind of the North Carolina planter

Nathaniel Macon. It is interesting, however, that despite the British orders the market for cotton was rapidly increasing both in quantity exported and in geographical area. The declining price was a long-term phenomenon only temporarily interrupted by the postwar prosperity, rather than a result of British restrictions. Statistics on the export of tobacco similarly give no real indication that the British orders in council were responsible for the constriction in markets or the drop in prices.

It is true, however, that the opinion that British restrictions were responsible for lower prices, even if unjustified, seems to have been widely held in the South. Margaret Kinard Latimer has recently brought to light evidence that this was a major factor in the demand for war at least in South Carolina. "Whether or not fighting a war with England," she concludes, "was the logical step to take as a remedy to the commercial and thus agricultural distress is not the question — the South Carolinians of 1812 were convinced that a war would help." Yet this leaves unanswered the question of why South Carolinians preferred to ignore the probability that war would further disrupt their commerce, while others, notably the New Englanders, were so painfully aware of it. It is possible that those South Carolina politicians who stressed the cotton depression as a cause for war were merely supplying additional reasons that might influence the wavering?

It must also be remembered that the decline in prices was not universal. Prices for beef, corn, and flour, the main exports of the Middle Atlantic states, actually increased over the decade, while the price of pork declined only slightly. In 1810-11 total exports in these products nearly doubled as American farms fed the Duke of Wellington's army in Spain. Pennsylvania, which voted sixteen to two for war with England, can hardly have been following the dictates of economic interest.

The South and the Middle Atlantic states, whose Congressmen furnished the major support for war, had little to gain economically from the conflict. Their direct trade in agricultural products was scarcely affected by the orders in council, and England had long been the major foreign market for both sections. Indeed, it might even be argued that these sections stood to lose as much by war as did New England. When, therefore, Nathaniel Macon spoke of going to war "to obtain the privilege of carrying the produce of our lands to a market" — an oft-quoted passage — he undoubtedly had in mind the "privilege" as much as the trade. Southerners went to war primarily to defend their rights, not their purses.

This is not to deny that economic factors were present. The final synthesis of the causes of the war will have to take into account various material factors — the fear of an Indian conspiracy in the West, for instance, and the concern over declining prices in the South — but it will also have to recognize that none of these economic theses furnishes a satisfactory explanation for the general demand for war. The only unifying factor, present in all sections of the country, was the growing feeling of patriotism, the realization that something must be done to vindicate the national honor. In recent years historians have tended more and more to stress this factor, particularly in its influence on the West, where a feeling of national pride was an obvious concomitant of the youth and exuberance of that section. Even Julius W. Pratt admitted that the war fever in the West "was doubtless due to various causes —

perhaps most of all to sheer exasperation at the long continued dilatory fashion of handling the nation's foreign affairs." This factor was probably even more important in the Middle Atlantic states and in the South where fewer material interests were at stake.

The system of commercial retaliation itself had not been defended on economic grounds. The first nonintercourse resolution had been introduced in the spring of 1806 by a Pennsylvanian, Andrew Gregg, as an instrument for gaining by peaceful means some recognition of America's neutral rights. The embargo and the later nonintercourse laws were intended to furnish the President with a lever of negotiation, to maintain the national dignity short of war. It was the growing disillusionment with this system, the growing feeling that war was the only means for maintaining the nation's integrity that eventually brought on the conflict. This mental conversion is aptly illustrated by the following letter of John Clopton of Virginia:

Let us consider what our government has done — how long it has borne with the repeated injuries which have been touched on in this letter — how often negotiations have been resorted to for the purpose of avoiding war; and the aggressions, instead of having been in any measure relaxed have been pursued with aggravating violence without a single ray of expectation that there exists any sore of disposition in the B[ritish] Cabinet to relax, but the strongest disposition to persist in their career.

. . . The outrages in impressing American seamen exceed all manner of description. Indeed the whole system of aggression now is such that the real question between G. Britain and the U. States has ceased to be a question merely relating to certain rights of commerce about which speculative politicians, might differ in opinion — it is now

clearly, positively, and directly *a question of independence,* that is to say, whether the U. States are really an independent nation.

Not all Republicans came to a similar conclusion at the same time. The process was a gradual one, beginning with the *Chesapeake* affair and the failure of the embargo to secure a recognition of American rights. The prominent Virginia Republican, Wilson Cary Nicholas, was one of the first to conclude that war was inevitable. Shortly after the Randolph schism in 1806, Nicholas had entered Congress at the behest of Jefferson, who needed an able floor leader in the House. The failure of the embargo convinced him that the whole policy of commercial retaliation was unsound, for it could not be enforced effectively enough to coerce the belligerents and it resulted only in the ruin of American agriculture. Since the Madison administration was unwilling to abandon the policy, Nicholas, rather than go into opposition, resigned his seat in the autumn of 1809. "We have tried negotiation until it is disgraceful to think of renewing it," he wrote Jefferson. "Commercial restrictions have been so managed as to operate only to our own injury. War then or submission only remain. In deciding between them I cannot hesitate a moment." George Washington Campbell of Tennessee reached a similar conclusion shortly after the *Chesapeake* affair, and he became one of the leading advocates for military preparations in the Tenth and Eleventh Congresses.

The gradual realization of the need for a more militant foreign policy was also reflected in the prominent Republican newspapers. Thomas Ritchie of the Richmond *Enquirer* considered the embargo the only honorable alternative to war, and when it was repealed Ritchie and the *Enquirer* began openly advocating war with England. William Duane, editor of the Philadelphia *Aurora*, generally supported the system of commercial retaliation, but the repudiation of David Erskine's agreement and the mission of Francis "Copenhagen" Jackson in the fall of 1809 convinced him that Britain did not intend to negotiate the question of neutral rights. By December 1809 he was advocating military preparations, the arming of American merchant ships, and, if those measures failed to intimidate Britain, "defensive war."

The old Jeffersonian, Nathaniel Macon, struggled long and valiantly with his conscience in an effort to reconcile Republican dogma with the obvious need for a vigorous defense of American rights. Throughout the Eleventh Congress he had been one of the administration leaders in the House, yet his basic conservatism was frequently evident. In the spring of 1810 he co-operated with John Randolph's efforts to reduce the size of the army and navy, even advocating that they be abolished altogether. As chairman of the foreign relations committee, Macon reported the nonintercourse bill of April 1810, known as Macon's Bill Number Two, but he personally opposed it because he felt it too provocative. Not until the beginning of the Twelfth Congress did he reach the conclusion that war was the only alternative. War was justified, he told the House in December 1811, because of the recent British seizures of ships carrying American agricultural products. This new aggression, he felt, showed that the British, instead of becoming more lenient, were actually tightening their system, and that further negotiation was useless. Macon thereafter co-operated with the war hawks but with some reluctance and with an occasional lapse. He voted against every effort to increase the size of the navy, and he consistently opposed all efforts during the session to raise the taxes to finance the war.

A number of Republicans, though they co-operated with the preparedness measures of the war hawks, could not make up their minds on the basic issue of peace or war until the last minute. As late as May 1812 a Massachusetts Federalist reported, perhaps somewhat wishfully, that a majority of the Virginia delegation was still against war. Besides the Federalists and the Quids, Randolph and Gray, he listed Taliaferro, Nelson, William A. Burwell, John Smith, and Matthew Clay as opposed to war. Representative of this group was Hugh Nelson. Nelson had been elected in 1811, but entered the Twelfth Congress with a lingering sympathy for the old Republican "minority" whose leader was John Randolph of Roanoke and whose prophet was John Taylor of Caroline. "I am a messmate of J[ohn] R[andolph]," he wrote to a friend in Charlottesville shortly after his arrival in Washington. "The more I see him the more I like him. He is as honest as the sun, with all his foibles, and as much traduced I believe as any man has ever been.... Do not be surprised if before the session closes I am classified with him as a minority man." Nelson's maiden speech in the House came on the resolution to increase the size of the regular army. It was a rehash of all the old Republican antiwar arguments — war would centralize the government, strengthen the executive, burden the people with taxes, armies, and navies, undermine our "republican simplicity," and subvert the Constitution. "I care not for the prices of cotton and tobacco as compared with the Constitution," he averred.

Moreover he felt it unlikely that the United States could ever gain recognition of her neutral rights, particularly since the only program the war hawks suggested was a territorial war begun by an invasion of Canada. Canada could not be conquered, but even if it could, would this enforce our rights? "Certainly not. The way to enforce these rights was by way of a great maritime force, which the nation were incompetent to raise and support." Nelson nevertheless felt the country should prepare for any evenutality because unless Britain relented there was no alternative to war. "I shall vote for the increase of the regular force," he concluded, "to go hand in hand with my friends, even in a war, if necessary and just." The most important of these friends was Nelson's neighbor from Charlottesville, Secretary of State Monroe, who by the spring of 1812 was a vigorous advocate of strong measures. In June, John Randolph wrote to John Taylor of Caroline that Monroe was "most furiously warlike & carries the real strength of the Southern representation with him."

Even more important than the personal influence of Monroe was the stimulus provided by President Madison. Most of the conservatives considered themselves loyal Republicans and were accustomed to following Presidential leadership in dealing with Britain and France. The policy of commercial retaliation had been largely an administration measure, and when the Twelfth Congress assembled in November 1811 Congress naturally looked to the Executive for guidance. Madison not only encouraged the war fever but he co-operated with the war hawks to a degree that has only recently begun to be fully recognized. His Annual Message to Congress in November 1811 outlined a program of

military and naval preparations that was adopted virtually intact by the war hawks. His release of the correspondence of Captain John Henry in March 1812[1] and his request in April for a thirty-day embargo as a prelude to war have been interpreted by his most recent biographer, Irving Brant, as attempts to stimulate the war sentiment in Congress.

The war hawks took full advantage of these moves by the President in their efforts to hold the conservatives in line. In the later stages of the session, when a number of Republicans began to get cold feet, the war hawks informed them that it was too late to back out. When in April the bill initiating a temporary embargo was reported for debate, Henry Clay warned the House that if it stopped now after all the war measures it had passed, it would cover itself "with shame and indelible disgrace." That this argument was effective is indicated by John Smilie, who followed Clay on the floor. Smilie, whose western-Pennsylvania Republicanism dated back to the fight over the Constitution in 1787, admitted that from the beginning of the session he had only reluctantly voted for the various proposals of the war hawks. He actually preferred continuing commercial retaliation to a war and an army of 25,000. But he realized it was too late to back down now; the nation's honor was at stake: "If we now recede we shall be a reproach to all nations."

Added to this internal stimulus was the pressure of continuing British intransigence. On May 22 dispatches arrived in Washington from British Foreign Secre-

[1] Capt. Henry was a British secret agent who had reported to Governor Craig of Canada on the discontent in New England during the time of the embargo. In February 1812 Henry, through the agency of a [self-styled] French nobleman, Count Crillon, sold his evidence of the disaffection in New England to the American State Department for $50,000.

tary Lord Castlereagh that contained nothing but a restatement of the British position. President Madison himself concluded that this was the last formal notice intended by the British government and sent his war message to Congress on June 1. It is not difficult to conceive that many a reluctant Republican came to the same decision.

It was thus with mixed motives that a majority of Republicans followed the war hawks to war. It is nevertheless clear that a primary factor in the mind of each was the conclusion that the only alternative to war was submission to the British commercial system. The balance of power in the House was held by men who had been in Congress for years, who had tried every expedient short of war to secure a recognition of American rights, and who at last had become surfeited with British commercial regulations. The war hawks, it is true, provided with their skill and energy the necessary impetus to war, but they could not have done so had not a majority of the Republican Party, particularly in the South, become gradually converted to the idea that war was the only alternative to national humiliation and disgrace. In this sense the war hawks acted as the intangible catalyst for a reaction whose basic elements were already present.

REGINALD HORSMAN, an Englishman now teaching in the United States, divided his graduate study between the two countries. In England, he studied British attitudes toward the orders in council. In America, he was a pupil of America. In an omitted portion of the article reproduced below, he summarizes the various interpretations of Western war spirit. Then he goes on to weigh the importance of the Indian menace and to cast the demands for the conquest of Canada in a broader frame than has been done by his predecessors.*

► ## The Conquest of Canada a Tactical Objective

In reading works such as Pratt it is possible to obtain the impression that the War Hawks talked constantly of Canada and of the Indians, and ignored maritime questions. This was not the case; by far the greater part of the argument of the War Hawks was devoted to attacking British maritime depredations. They had a material interest in doing this, and what is more they had a genuine feeling that American national honor was suffering from British action at sea. Many of these men were young and proud, and were willing to combine the principles of self-interest and honor. They felt anger at the British regulations which they thought had produced the commercial distress, and they felt anger at all the other British infringements of American rights. Only a quarter of a century before, the United States had struggled for independence against a country which now ignored this new-won freedom. The leaders of these War Hawks were young men who had been raised on the traditions of the War of Independence. The older generation, well represented by Jefferson and Madison, were "first generation revolutionaries" — men who had gambled for independence, had won, and were in their later years little inclined to risk their winnings in an uncertain war with England. Henry Clay and his young allies were the "second generation revolutionaries" — young men who were

*Reginald Horsman, "Western War Aims, 1811-1812," *Indiana Magazine of History*, vol. LIII (1957), pp. 9-18. Reprinted with the permission of the *Indiana Magazine of History*.

willing to take chances with the hard-won gains of their parents. They had grown to manhood hearing oft-repeated tales of the War of Independence, but they themselves had long been compelled to suffer without retaliation the constant infringement of American rights. The generation of the War Hawks had come of age during a period in which American seamen were being taken from American ships, and in which Britain had attempted to tell America how and what she should export. It is not surprising that when to these acts was added growing agricultural distress there was an ever-increasing cry for war.

The report of the Foreign Relations Committee of November 29, 1811, recommending war preparations for the United States, concerned itself exclusively with maritime matters. This report, which bluntly stated that the time for submission was at an end, objected bitterly to British commercial regulations and to the practice of impressment. It summarized the essential cause of complaint against Great Britain with the argument that the United States claimed the right to export her products without losing either ships or men. The arguments of the War Hawks in the ensuing debates clearly followed the lines of reasoning laid down in this report. Their leaders agreed that war was necessary against Britain for the defense of American maritime interests and honor. Richard M. Johnson of Kentucky speaking on December 11, 1811, certainly discussed Canada, but previously he had stated: "Before we relinquish the conflict, I wish to see Great Britain renounce the piratical system of paper blockade; to liberate our captured seamen on board her ships of war; relinquish the practice of impressment on board our merchant vessels; to repeal her Orders in Council;

and cease, in every other respect, to violate our neutral rights; to treat us as an independent people."

In speech after speech the War Hawks echoed Johnson's sentiments. Orders in Council, illegal blockades, impressment, and the general terms of neutral rights and national honor dominated their arguments. Clay himself stated on December 31, 1811: "What are we not to lose by peace? — commerce, character, a nation's best treasure, honor!" Clay's whole argument in this speech was for the necessity of war to defend American maritime rights.

The letters of the War Hawks appear to support their public utterances. George W. Campbell, Senator from Tennessee, wrote to Andrew Jackson that it is "difficult to percieve [*sic*] how war can be avoided, without degrading the national character, still lower.... For there is no ground to expect G. Britain will abandon her system of depredation on our commerce, or her habitual violations of the personal rights of our citizens in the impressment of our seamen." George M. Troup of Georgia wrote to Governor David B. Mitchell on February 12, 1812, denouncing all further temporizing or indecision. He wanted either war or an open abandonment of the contest — nothing else would satisfy the just expectations of the southern people, "who have been bearing the brunt of the restrictive system from the beginning." William Lowndes of South Carolina was confident in December, 1811, that unless England repealed her Orders in Council, there would be war before the end of the session. These westerners and southerners were vitally interested in maritime questions, and showed a very real awareness of the long years of British depredations upon American commerce....

There is no doubt that the presence of hostile Indians on the frontier was of great importance to the westerners. Any careful study of the records of this period inevitably leads one to that conclusion. The debates of the Twelfth Congress and the territorial papers of Indiana, Michigan, and Louisiana-Missouri, have constant references to the Indian problem. One has only to read the letters of Governor William Henry Harrison of Indiana to the War Department to realize the extent to which the thinking of certain areas of the West was dominated by this factor.

Even more important from the point of view of this study is that there was no doubt in the minds of the settlers that the British were instigating the action of the Indians. . . . [But the] fact that the frontiersmen connected the British and the Indians is no reason for supposing that the prevention of this alliance was the *dominating* motive in the vote of Congress for war in 1812. This view fails to take into consideration several relevant facts. In the first place, the core of the feeling against the Indians was in the exposed northwest frontier — in the Indiana, Michigan, and Illinois territories, and it should be remembered that these areas had no vote in Congress. It is true, of course, that the anger against the supposed British inciting of the Indians was felt deeply outside the immediately exposed area — Kentucky was much incensed at the Indian depredations and Kentuckians fought and were killed at Tippecanoe; also Andrew Jackson wrote from Tennessee offering Harrison the use of his forces after that encounter. Yet, it is essential to realize that of the 79 votes for war in the House only a total of nine votes came from the states of Kentucky, Tennessee, and Ohio, while a total of 37 came from the South

Atlantic states of Maryland, Virginia, North and South Carolina, and Georgia. Pennsylvania, a state of limited frontier area by this period, alone provided 16 votes for war. There is no doubt that the *leaders* of the movement for war were often westerners, whether from the Ohio Valley, frontier New Hampshire, or western New York, but the actual vote for war depended on non-frontiersmen. The Indian menace undoubtedly influenced frontier areas, and in some was the dominating factor, but it seems unlikely that the large vote for war in non-frontier areas was inspired by a desire to protect the northwest frontier from Indian depredations. The importance of the argument concerning Indians in the Congressional debates of 1811 and 1812 has been greatly overestimated. British encouragement of the Indians was discussed in the war debates but it was discussed in connection with other factors. A reference to the murderous savages urged on by the British provided a fine emotional climax to any speech, but it would appear that the argument which united the 79 representatives of diverse sections to vote for war was the more generally applicable one of the need to sell produce in order to live. . . .

Burt, in his detailed work on Britain, America, and Canada, suggests, without detailed elaboration, that the conquest of Canada was anticipated as the seizure of a hostage rather than as the capture of a prize. It would seem from the debates in Congress that this was indeed the case. The key fact is that almost exclusively in their speeches the War Hawks first considered the *reasons* why war was necessary, and dwelt on maritime grievances, and then, when turning to the *methods* of waging war, discussed the question of invading Canada. It is true that the war party saw in the conquest of Canada an opportunity to prevent further Indian depredations, but there seems no reason to believe that this was in itself a sufficient reason for the war party to achieve such general support in 1812. The various sections of the United States were not sufficiently altruistic for the South Atlantic states to demand war and the conquest of Canada for the purpose of relieving the Northwest from Indian attacks. Yet, the demand for Canada entered into the speeches of the southerners as it did into the speeches of the western War Hawks. . . .

Calhoun, the young South Carolinian, clearly stated the reasons for southern support of Canadian conquest, and helped to explain the general attitude of the war party, in a speech on December 12, 1811. In answering Randolph's taunt that the Canadas bore no relation to American shipping and maritime rights he stated: "By his system, if you receive a blow on the breast, you dare not return it on the head; you are obliged to measure and return it on the precise point on which it was received. If you do not proceed with mathematical accuracy, it ceases to be just self-defence; it becomes an unprovoked attack." This gives the essence of the matter. Once the War Hawks had decided they wanted war, they were obliged to face the problem of where they could injure their mighty foe. At sea it seemed that there was little hope. Britain's vast navy, which had swept France from the seas, was to be matched against a handful of American frigates. Apart from the activities of American privateers there seemed little hope of waging effective war against Britain on the sea. The conquest of Canada was the obvious, if not the only method of injuring Britain. Clay's speech of February 22, 1810, has been quoted as

one of the first appeals for the conquest of Canada: "The conquest of Canada is in your power" are words of joy to the expansionist historian. Yet these words were said after Clay had discussed British mercantile spoilations, and after he had stated that as peaceful measures had failed it was time for resistance by the sword. He then tried to convince the weak and vacillating Eleventh Congress that war against Great Britain was practicable, and that injury could be inflicted upon their enemy: "It is said, however, that no object is attainable by war with Great Britain. In its fortunes, we are to estimate not only the benefit to be derived to ourselves, but the injury to be done the enemy. The conquest of Canada is in your power."

Members of the war party in the Twelfth Congress echoed these words of Clay. Two representatives of North Carolina — Israel Pickens and William R. King — summarized the essential reasoning behind the demand for Canada. King on December 13, 1811, stated that he was not enamored of conquest but that this war had been forced upon America: "We cannot, under existing circumstances, avoid it. To wound our enemy in the most vulnerable part should only be considered." Pickens, less than a month later, answered the opposition that though the contemplated attack on the British Provinces is called a war of offense, "when it is considered as the only mode in our reach, for defending rights universally recognised and avowedly violated, its character is changed." Even calm and honest Nathaniel Macon of Virginia [North Carolina], whose opinion can surely be given as much weight as the impassioned and half-mad Randolph of the same state, contended that the war which the United States was about to enter was not a war of conquest — "Its object is to obtain the privilege of carrying the produce of our lands to a market" — but he considered that no war could long continue to be merely one of defense. The War Hawks called for attack upon Canada because it was the only certain way they knew of attacking Britain.

Peaceful restriction had apparently failed and the West and South resolved to fight the British in the only area in which she appeared to be vulnerable, her North American provinces. Perhaps the most adequate summary by a westerner of why the West wanted to fight was that given by Andrew Jackson on March 12, 1812, when, as commander of the militia of the western district of Tennessee, he issued a call for volunteers from this area. In this document, if in no other, one would expect to see reflected the ideas and aspirations of the people of the West; a commander calling for volunteers does not use unpopular arguments. Under the heading, "For what are we going to fight?", Jackson wrote these words: "We are going to fight for the reestablishment of our national charactor [sic], misunderstood and vilified at home and abroad; for the protection of our maritime citizens, impressed on board British ships of war and compelled to fight the battles of our enemies against ourselves; to vindicate our right to a free trade, and open a market for the productions of our soil, now perishing on our hands because the *mistress of the ocean* has forbid us to carry them to any foreign nation; in fine, to seek some indemnity for past injuries, some security against future aggressions, by the conquest of all the British dominions upon the continent of north america."

The coming of war in 1812 was not a sudden event; it was the culmination of a long series of injuries and insults, of checks to American commerce, and of the infringement of American rights. The United States, under the leadership of Jefferson and Madison, repeatedly attempted to defend her rights by peaceful economic coercion. Yet, almost inevitably, a breaking point was reached. The time came when, with national honor at its lowest ebb, and large sections of agricultural America suffering depression, any war seemed preferable to a dishonorable and unprofitable peace. The young War Hawks who urged war in 1811 and 1812 had grown up in this atmosphere of the oppression of American rights, and with apparently nothing to gain by peace, urged America to fight for the right to exist as a fully independent nation. Considering the period through which they had grown to manhood, it is not surprising that they demanded war to preserve American commerce, neutral rights, and honor, and that, in order to revenge themselves upon their enemy, they proposed the invasion of Canada. The suspected British instigation of the Indians was an added irritant, but if Great Britain had pursued a conciliatory maritime policy towards the United States, it seems extremely unlikely that there would have been war between the two countries. The fundamental cause of the War of 1812 was the British maritime policy which hurt both the national pride and the commerce of the United States.

IRVING BRANT, a Pulitzer-Prize–winning
newspaperman, devoted many years to a six-volume
life of James Madison. This work is frankly designed
to refurbish the somewhat tarnished reputation of
the fourth President of the United States. The first
passage below discusses the administration's role in the
passage of an embargo act in March 1812. The
second passage attempts to explain Madison's final
decision in favor of war. The critical factor, as Brant
sees it, was the President's receipt of a communication
from the British foreign secretary, Lord Castlereagh,
which seemed to indicate that the orders in council
would be obdurately defended.*

Madison Encouraged the War Movement

On March 30 the House Committee on Foreign Affairs adopted a resolution informing Secretary Monroe that it was ready to proceed with the measures expected by the people and would "be happy to be informed when, in the opinion of the Executive, the measures of preparation will be in such forwardness as to justify the step contemplated." A secret session was arranged for next day. Committeeman John Randolph, saying he would not be bound to secrecy, took notes of the meeting and read from them in the House debate — a fact which serves to identify his full memorandum in the papers of Senator Smith of Maryland. The President's position was stated in the opening sentence:

"March 31. Colonel Monroe attended the committee: he said the Executive was of the same opinion that it entertained at the beginning of the session, 'that without an accommodation with Great Britain Congress ought to declare war before adjourning.' "

The unprepared state of the country, Monroe continued, was the reason for not taking that step at once. The communications from Foster afforded no hope of an adjustment and the period had arrived for decisive action. An em-

*From *James Madison: The President, 1809-1812*, by Irving Brant, pp. 426-431, 478-483, copyright © 1956 by The Bobbs-Merrill Company, Inc., reprinted by special permission of the publishers.

bargo not exceeding sixty days, "as preparatory to war," had been spoken of. "Without war, public expectations would be defeated and our character destroyed abroad."

The time contemplated by the Executive for a declaration was the return of the *Hornet* [with the latest news from London and Paris]. "It was very desirable to know how we stood with France." Justice from her would increase the pressure on England. Injustice would require a "resort to measures against her also." Monroe then made a specific proposal which still encompassed the possibility of peace:

"No immediate declaration of war being contemplated, an embargo of sixty days, within which time the Hornet must return, will leave the ultimate policy of the government in our hands."

During the embargo period, the Secretary said, merchants could arm their ships and tax bills could be passed. By increasing imposts, as Gallatin requested, Congress could avoid stamp and distillery taxes for the present year. To speed the raising of the new army the President would like to enlist 15,000 out of the 25,000 regulars for only eighteen months. And he wished to know the sentiments of Congress on the embargo.

Smilie of Pennsylvania, close to the administration, said there was a pretty strong inclination to the measure. Chairman Porter was afraid that a premature declaration of war would lead to defeats, disgrace and discontent. He favored a short adjournment of Congress, to be followed by an embargo preparatory to war. Calhoun disagreed:

"'Some decisive measure is required that would give a tone to our legislation which has not been hitherto perceived. That meas-

ure in his opinion would be an embargo. Asked Monroe if we expected to take Quebec this campaign."

Monroe answered no and presented a query from Gallatin. If the loan should fail, would Congress adopt other measures to facilitate the raising of money? "We will give facilities one way or another," replied Calhoun. Then, said Monroe, "the only question is whether to lay the embargo now or to defer it."

"Will the Executive recommend it by special message?" asked Harper of New Hampshire. Monroe: "If you give me the necessary assurance that it will be acceptable to the House, the Executive will recommend it."

War, the Secretary of State went on, would produce effects by stimulating the spirit of patriotism. Injuries that might be sustained by a particular part of the Union (the seaboard) would not affect the nation at large. But "the Executive will not take upon itself the responsibility of declaring that we are prepared for war" The committee then declared for the embargo. Monroe promised to bring back the President's opinion next day.

Before nightfall, Madison lost the faint hope he cherished of a change in British policies through the expiration of parliamentary restrictions on the Prince Regent. News came via London papers that the regent was retaining a cabinet so conservative that Grenville and Grey refused to join it. Wellesley was to be replaced by Castlereagh — a leap from the frying pan to a dull fire. Hearing of a sudden speed-up of embargo plans, Minister Sérurier sought the cause that evening and was told that the effect of the Prince Regent's action was decisive — embargo now and war in sixty days. "The administration has chosen its course completely," he reported. As Madison himself (three days later) described the London news and his own action:

"It appears that Perceval, etc., are to retain their places and that they prefer war with us to a repeal of their Orders in Council. We have nothing left therefore, but to make ready for it. As a step to it an embargo for sixty days was recommended to Congress."

The step thus described by the President as a step to war was asked of Congress in a confidential message of April 1. Barely taking time to leave the room, the House Foreign Affairs Committee presented an embargo bill "drafted according to the wishes and directions of the Secretary of the Treasury." Answering queries, Grundy and Speaker Clay both termed it a measure leading directly to war. "We know," said Clay, "no pains have been spared to vilify the government," but by proceeding now, Congress would win the support of people who had previously been willfully blinded:

"It remains for us to say whether we will shrink or follow up the patriotic conduct of the President. As an American and a member of this House, he felt a pride that the Executive had recommended this measure."

This stirred the anger of John Randolph, the antiwar member of the Foreign Relations Committee. "He was confident in declaring that this was not a measure of the Executive" — it was something engendered on him by the extensive excitement of newspapers, both ministerial and Federalist, and would be extended and extended:

"At the end of sixty days we shall not have war, and the reason is, the Executive dare not plunge the nation into a war in our unprepared state. He had too much reliance on his wisdom and virtue to believe that he

would be guilty of such gross and unparalleled treason."

Coming from Randolph, such a personal attack could be ignored. Not so when Seybert of Pennsylvania, who favored the embargo as a precursor to war, said he had information from a trusted friend that the President did not intend offensive operations. The veteran Smilie, described by Foster as "most in the confidence of the President," challenged his colleague's statement:

"He had heard but one sentiment from the President, which is *that we must make war* unless Great Britain relents. The President had always supposed that the embargo must precede war—the only difference has been as to the time, which has been finally compromised. The embargo is intended as a war measure. He would assure his colleagues it was [so] intended by both the Executive and the Committee of Foreign Relations."

The bill passed the House in an evening session, 70 to 41, on the day the President sent his message. Commenting two days later, with the Senate's action uncertain, Madison observed that the embargo would "add fuel to party discontent and interested clamor," but he regarded it as a rational and provident measure, which would be "relished by a greater portion of the nation than an omission of it." Could the step have been taken earlier and for three or four months, it might have alarmed the British cabinet for their Peninsular armies, leading to concessions. It could not be foretold whether a sixty-day embargo could produce that result "before the sword is stained with blood," but such an effect was not be counted on.

The Senate lengthened the embargo to ninety days and passed it; the House accepted the amendment. The President signed the bill three days after he asked for it. The lengthening, Madison reported, "proceeded from the united votes of those who wished to make it a negotiating instead of a war measure, of those who wished to put off the day of war as long as possible... and of those whose mercantile constituents had ships abroad." Some also desired the extension "as a ruse against the enemy," hoping for a declaration of war before the embargo expired....

[From March through May the nation waited, hoping for good news from abroad and strengthening its military preparations. At the end of May, the British minister, Augustus J. Foster, presented instructions from his superior, written in April, that seemed to end the hope of British concessions. On June 1, Madison sent a war message to Congress, and on June 18 the war began. Unbeknownst to the Americans, the Orders in Council, their greatest complaint against England, were repealed at almost the same time.]

On May 11 Prime Minister Spencer Perceval, stubborn supporter of the Orders in Council, was shot to death by a maniac. With manufacturers clamoring against the orders and with committees of Parliament piling up proof of the damage they were inflicting on Great Britain, the cabinet was forced to resign. News of the American embargo awakened the interim government to the imminence of war. On June 16 House Leader Castlereagh reluctantly announced that the Orders in Council would be suspended. They were abandoned next day — the day on which the Senate completed the American decision to go to war against them.

Speaker Clay was "far from acknowledging," in later House debate, that knowledge of repeal of the Orders in

Council would have prevented a declaration of war — he regarded impressment of seamen as a much more serious aggression. Madison, in retrospect, thought the time element decisive. The United States, he told Jared Sparks in 1830, had repeatedly declared the absolute necessity of repealing the orders before any terms of entire conciliation could be made. So when Castlereagh's letter was presented, positively affirming that the orders would not be rescinded, it could only be looked on "as intended to show an utter disregard of the complaints of the United States ... shut[ting] out all prospects of conciliation." The President consequently recommended war.

"Had Castlereagh's letter therefore been of a different tone [said Madison] war would not have been at that time declared, nor is it probable that it would have followed, because there was every prospect that the affair of impressment and other grievances might have been reconciled after the repeal of the obnoxious Orders in Council."

This accords with a fact that permeates the contemporary record — that although Madison worked to move Congress and the nation *toward* war, he never committed himself so completely to it that repeal of the Orders in Council would not have halted the movement. It accords no less with the account given by the man closest to him during this period, his private secretary Edward Coles, who was asked whether it was true that Madison was forced into the War of 1812 by popular influence or congressional pressure.

"It was congenial alike to the life and character of Mr. Madison," Coles wrote to William C. Rives in 1856, "that he should be reluctant to go to war." He would not "resort to this savage and brutal manner of settling disputes between nations" while a hope remained of maintaining national interest and honor by diplomacy. The President did not "entirely despair of preserving peace" until the British government "contended that France must not only repeal her decrees against us, but against all the world," before England would repeal or modify her orders. This "closed the door to peace in Mr. Madison's opinion," and from that time his mind was "irrevocably fixed on war as the only course left us" by Britain's conduct. That carries the decision, with almost total finality, back to July 23, 1811, when Madison rejected Foster's demand for universal repeal. Monroe made a similar diagnosis in the week of the declaration of war, telling Colonel Taylor that nothing would satisfy the British ministry short of unconditional submission:

"This fact being completely ascertained the only remaining alternative was to get ready for fighting, and to begin as soon as we were ready. This was the plan of the administration when Congress met in December [November] last; the President's message announced it; and every step taken by the administration since has led to it."

Edward Coles described the President's strategy from November to June. "A class of irritable men," eager for war, thought Madison and other prudent leaders too tolerant. They saw no need of military preparations. "Let one drop they said of American blood be shed and it would fill our ranks with men, and our Treasury with loans." These "hotspurs of the day" were opposed by a number of "sound, prudent and patriotic men" who wished to avoid war if possible, and to carry it on, if it proved unavoidable, with honor and advantage to the country. Another diplomatic effort for peace, they contended, was not only proper in itself but would give time to put the nation in shape for war if it should ulti-

mately take place. The President, standing between these two groups, had "a strong conviction" that for the sake of national strength and international standing, "the war should be declared by a large and influential majority." To that end he shaped his course:

"He endeavored to moderate the zeal and impatience of the ultra belligerent men, and to stimulate the more moderate and forbearing. To check those who were anxious to rush on hastily to extreme measures without due preparation and to urge those who lagged too far behind."

This, said Coles, Madison tried to do without harshly curbing one group, and by ardent and forcible appeals to the other, giving time for powerful popular sentiment to have its influence, "not on him as has been asserted, but on the tardy and over cautious members of Congress." By this course he increased the vote for war in the two houses and added to the popularity of it, "though it would seem by so doing he had brought into question the ardor and sincerity of his own conduct."

Cole's criticisms of unthinking hotspurs did not apply to the most prominent War Hawks. Speaker Clay, who did more than any other man in Congress to invigorate its war spirit, took the same stand as Madison on the delay of a declaration till preparations were advanced and England had time to reappraise her policies. Calhoun said the objection to an immediate declaration was obvious, "we are not yet prepared." Cheves's attempt to build up the Navy had similar implications. Johnson and Harper were in close sympathy with the President. Grundy, on the other hand, led a party seeking immediate war and displayed an air of truculent uncertainty regarding Madison, while Ringgold of Maryland, according to Minister Foster, carried the draft of a declaration in his pocket until it was worn out.

As President, during the critical period from March 1809 to June 1812, Madison pursued a course of which the American people had scarcely an inkling. They were totally unaware, as was Congress, that in his first month in office he sent word to the British government that adherence to the Orders in Council would mean war with the United States; that repeal of them, unless France acted similarly, would lead to Franco-American hostilities.

Madison's foreign policy presented an olive branch backed by a sword. Over and over, in the three-year period, he offered to England the alternatives of war with the United States or a partnership against Napoleon, committing the country (as he finally told Congress in his war message) as far as he could within his constitutional powers. France was offered a similar prospect of united action against England, conditioned on a change of conduct by France alone. In the ensuing developments British adherence to the Orders in Council brought war, while Napoleon's shifting tactics of maritime aggression left him as a vexatious obstacle to the free development of American policy. At no time was Madison deceived by an imperial system under which American vessels were burned at sea instead of being captured under French decree. But, the decrees being technically revoked, it suited the legal basis of the President's position toward Britain to treat them in that light. Had not England been inflicting deeper wounds on American independence, economic welfare and national spirit, the outrages committed by Bonaparte would have led inevitably to war with France.

In his original offer of an American partnership to either European belligerent that would take steps to earn it Madison demonstrated his freedom from the partisan charge of subserviency to France. He also showed himself to be a hard realist, seeking national advantage and ignoring the ultimate implications of the struggle going on in Europe. It was enough for him that the United States was thought able to defend itself against Napoleon, whatever happened in the Old World, and that England had but to drop her commercial and naval aggressions in order to obtain an American ally instead of a foe.

For the failure of diplomacy to avert war there were many causes. Most controllable, and least important, was the absence of an American minister from London during the crucial final year. Had Madison sent some clearsighted Federalist like Harrison Gray Otis to succeed Pinkney, there would have been no distrust of democracy or baseless suspicion of French influence to becloud his warnings of war unless the Orders in Council were repealed. Yet the similar warnings Otis published in London as a private citizen went quite unheeded — drowned in the roar of Federalist approval of England and denunciation of the Madison administration. Unable to speak for his own party, such a Federalist might have fared no better as a minister.

Those who actually spoke for that party — Pickering, Lowell, Quincy, the Massachusetts legislature and the Federalist press, together with their ally Randolph — did more than Madison or the War Hawks to bring on the conflict. By their active support of Great Britain and vituperation of their own government as corrupt and imbecile they created a dual delusion which poured on London in two lines of communication. Directly through the American press and with seeming verification in the dispatches of the credulous Augustus Foster the British cabinet heard of a French puppet in the White House vying with illiterate congressmen in the dissemination of meaningless threats.

Yet all these aids to error might have been overcome had not the British cabinet been headed by Spencer Perceval, who seemed to regard American commercial rivalry as a greater menace than Bonaparte. With foreign affairs in the hands of men like Wellesley and Castlereagh, who had no understanding of the United States or the likely effect of their own actions, the intransigence of the Prime Minister was ideally implemented for undesired and unexpected results. It could at least be said for France that the dictatorial blundering of Napoleon was opposed by his ministers to the limited extent of their daring. The British government had perfect teamwork in perversity.

President Madison to be successful in his diplomatic strategy needed to deal with men whose understanding matched his own. The absence of that quality in his opponents added force to a partisan opposition at home that overran the border of disloyalty. With that knowledge, but with faith in a deeper and broader spirit of devotion in the American people as a whole, the President turned to the waging of the war he asked Congress to declare — one that its supporters regarded as a second war of independence.

The most recent study of the coming of war in 1812 is *Prologue to War,* by the editor of this pamphlet, BRADFORD PERKINS. A diplomatic historian whose special interest is Anglo-American relations, the author stresses the breakdown of understanding between the two powers, the affronts to American national honor, and the partisan nature of the vote for war. In weighing Madison's role, he uses much the same evidence as Irving Brant but comes to quite different conclusions. Among other things, he minimizes the importance of Madison's embargo message.*

Madison Was a Failure

The President's embargo message . . . gave an illusory appearance of decisive leadership. Still, after a winter during which the White House had most closely resembled the oracle at Delphi, any appearance of forthrightness took on significance. Since his November message the President had pretty much kept his own counsel. In January, to expose England's rigidity, he submitted to Congress correspondence between Monroe and Foster; in March he made public the Henry letters, with consequences that reflected upon his good sense and harmed the war movement. Otherwise the President acted more like William McKinley in 1898 than James Knox Polk in 1846, and War

Hawks and peace men both claimed him. Republicans pleaded for a clear lead, and late in March several imploring letters reached the White House within a few days. The embargo message, an apparent answer to this prayer, did not convince suspicious men. In March John C. Calhoun temporarily abandoned his doubts of the administration, writing, "Their Zeal and intelligence can not now be doubted." Shortly after the message his doubts returned, and he commented, "Our President tho a man of amiable manners and great talents, has not I fear those commanding talents, which are necessary to controul those about him. . . . He reluctantly gives up

*Bradford Perkins, *Prologue to War, England and the United States, 1805-1812,* Berkeley and Los Angeles, 1961, pp. 378-382, 399-406, 425-426. Reprinted with the permission of the University of California Press.

the system of peace. It is to be hoped, that as war is now seriously determined on, the Executive department will move with much more vigour. Without it it is impossible for Congress to proceed." A single message extorted by demanding legislators could not destroy Madison's reputation for weakness.

Party doctrine and personal preference caused President Madison to follow a silent course. Republican constitutional theory glorified the legislature at the expense of the executive, providing an excuse for presidential silence on the question of war. This silence angered, among others, Speaker Clay, who bluntly told the administration: "Altho' the power of declaring War belongs to the Congress, I do not see that it falls less within the scope of the President's constitutional duty to recommend . . . measures . . . than any other which, being suggested by him, they alone can adopt." In dealing with legislative problems Madison showed none of the boldness, even rashness, that led him to accept the assurances of Erskine and Cadore. In the war session he did nothing to prevent preparedness legislation, but he also did far less than he might have done to encourage it. In pacific times this intelligent man might have been a successful president. But he was not cut in the heroic mold. *"Madison* may be *good,"* an editorialist commented, "but in a *national view,* there is a great distinction between *Good,* and GOOD ENOUGH." Left to himself, with a Congress like the Tenth, James Madison would have been a complete failure in 1812.

This is not to say that because he lacked determination when dealing with his Cabinet, his party, and the legislature the President took a cowardly, indecisive view of America's position. His enemies accused him of attempting to preserve the support of both War Hawks and peace men for the election of 1812 or, later, suggested that he supported war only after War Hawks threatened to prevent his reëlection. This was nonsense. Since the very beginning of the session Madison's analysis had been based upon more honorable grounds. It combined simplicity and complexity, optimism and pessimism in baffling degrees, but it was consistently maintained.

Toward the end of November Madison told Foster that for America "anything was better than remaining in such a state" as the existing one. (Madison naturally failed to add that the state of the nation owed much to his own activities as secretary of state and president.) If war became the only alternative, the President would face it. Summarizing his position, although characteristically bestowing the power of choice upon Congress and directing his musings to an American safely distant at St. Petersburg, the President wrote that the question "simply is, whether all the trade to which the orders [in Council] are . . . applied, is to be abandoned, or the hostile operation of them, be hostilely resisted. The apparent disposition is certainly not in favor of the first alternative, though it is more than probable, that if the second should be adopted, the execution of it will be put off till the close of the Session approaches." Not a single piece of reputable evidence suggests that the President abandoned this conviction at any time, although he reserved the right to decide later whether hostility should be shown with a fly whisk, a club, or a sword. When Foster described Monroe as "a mild moderate man, . . . with whom I am happy to say it has been my good fortune to be on the best terms," he really was indirectly comparing the Secretary and the less complaisant President. On

April 1, just at the time here being discussed, Foster scribbled in his diary, "go to the President's—He very warlike, calls our orders tantamount to Letters of marque." But if he spoke freely to Foster, Madison never made his position clear enough to give direction to Congress, and throughout the winter, while resignedly prepared to go to war, the President hoped for some acceptable solution to the nation's problems which would make war unnecessary.

As Bernard Mayo has observed, the President "seemed less intent upon harnessing the chariot of war than upon driving the old coach of diplomacy."[1] He combined warnings and invitations in his conversations with Foster. So frequent were his suggestions that Britain, without doing serious damage to herself, might modify her restrictions upon commerce in a way palatable to the United States, that Foster finally reported: "The name of the Orders in Council has become more objectionable to him than the substance." Undoubtedly the British envoy misunderstood Madison, who surely required benefits of substance as well as of form. On the other hand the Chief Executive would almost certainly have accepted an accommodation that did not concede all that some Americans desired. Even when he recommended an embargo to Congress, a step the political world interpreted as a harbinger of war, the President went out of his way to inform Foster that timely British concessions could prevent a declaration. Down to the very end, albeit with increasing pessimism, James Madison clung to a hope that commercial pressure and American war preparations would bring England to terms. . . .

[After the embargo, Congress and the

[1] Bernard Mayo, *Henry Clay, Spokesman of the New West*, Boston, 1937, p. 439.

President sat back to await the return of U.S.S. *Hornet,* which had been sent to Europe to bring the latest reports from London and Paris.] On May 22, weeks after she was expected and after, too, false reports of her arrival had thrown sessions of Congress into confusion, the *Hornet* arrived. Monroe's office became suffocatingly crowded as officials and citizens sought to learn if she brought any news that would enable America to escape gracefully from a war. The dispatches disappointed everyone. As Minister Sérurier received no instructions to guide him, and [minister] Joel Barlow's reports made it clear that Napoleon continued irascible, hope had to be abandoned for a settlement with France which would ease the path of war with Britain. Although unofficial accounts aplenty showed that the Orders in Council were being heavily attacked, [chargé] Russell's reports held out no prospect of repeal. Anger, confusion, and gloom spread through Washington. Sérurier had an uncomfortable conversation with Monroe when they met at Speaker Clay's, the Secretary complaining that the administration had been betrayed by France. There were reports that the Cabinet, which met on two consecutive days to discuss future policy, contained almost as many opinions as members. The *National Intelligencer,* however, insisted that England was the chief enemy — "let it not be said that the misconduct of France neutralizes in the least that of Great Britain" — and Monroe's conversations with Foster made it seem that there was nothing to hope from England.

Although not hostile in tone, Castlereagh's instructions to Foster, which formed the most important part of the *Hornet's* budget of information, showed how little Britain understood America. Basing his argument largely on a recent report by the Duke of Bassano, the Foreign Secretary declared it was now obvious, as England had maintained all along, that France had not repealed her decrees. America had been tricked.

It is impossible America should not feel under these Circumstances that She has not only an Act of Justice to perform by Great Britain, but that France has deliberately attached Conditions to the Repeal of Her Decrees which she knew Great Britain could never accept, hoping thereby to foment Disunion between Great Britain and America. America can never be justified in continuing to resent against Us that failure of Relief, which is alone attributable to the insidious Policy of the Enemy. ... we are entitled to claim at Her Hands, as an act not less of Policy, than Justice, ... that She could cease to Treat Great Britain as an Enemy.

The truth of this analysis of French policy seemed so obvious to Castlereagh that he expected the Americans to share it. He hoped the evidence of imperial perfidy would provide the United States with "an opportunity of receding without disgrace from the precipice of War. ... To rescue America from the influence of France, is of more importance, than committing Her to War with that Power." To sweeten the pill for America, Castlereagh offered to regulate licenses so that the two countries might share European trade, or even to abandon them entirely. "At any other time," as Theodore C. Smith has observed, "this would have at least opened the way for renewed negotiations, but not in 1812."[2] Castlereagh and his colleagues totally misread the situation in America. The instructions, far more pleading than threatening, actually determined Madison to abandon his hedging for peace.

[2] Theodore C. Smith, "War Guilt in 1812," *Massachusetts Historical Society, Proceedings*, vol. LXIV (1952), p. 338.

On May 27 and 28 Foster discussed the British argument and proposed concession with Monroe and Madison. The Americans ignored the proposal on licenses, to which they had formerly attached so much importance. They stubbornly reiterated that the Berlin and Milan decrees had been repealed. Seizing upon Castlereagh's declaration that England would insist upon complete, unconditional French repeal and abandonment of the municipal regulations shutting off British commerce with Europe, they declared this an extension of England's demands. "With this formal notice," Madison recalled fifteen years later, "no choice remained but between war and degradation, a degradation inviting fresh provocation & rendering war sooner or later inevitable." The Foreign Secretary's instructions, Madison told Jared Sparks in 1830, were "intended to show an utter disregard of the complaints of the United States. This letter seemed to shut out the prospects of conciliation, & the president considered war as the next necessary step to vindicate the rights and honor of the nation." The failure of understanding was reciprocal.

For more than a month eager members of the Foreign Affairs Committee had been drafting a manifesto for use as a reply to the presidential war message, and Monroe also prepared one for friendly congressmen. On May 13, when nearly a sixth of the membership was absent, the House of Representatives voted to recall absentees. On May 18 eighty Republicans caucused to arrange their plans, and three days later the President was reported at work on his war message. Apparently a congressional delegation headed by Clay visited the White House to assure Madison that Congress awaited his message, and later, on a morning ride to Georgetown, the Speaker told a colleague that the war message could be expected on June 1. On May 29 John Randolph delivered a bitter attack on the project. After he had accused the Republican leaders of seeking to make Americans "the tools, the minions, sycophants, parasites of France," he was silenced by the Speaker and Calhoun. Visitors began to examine Foster's livestock and even the marquee under which he held his famous parties, with an eye to purchasing them when he departed. Congress adjourned for the week end, knowing that on Monday the long-awaited climax of the battle between honor and interest would begin.

During these hectic days, last-minute misgivings plagued the administration. The President, who knew that he must go ahead and was prepared to do his duty, faced it without enthusiasm. On May 25 he sent Congress the discouraging correspondence from Barlow, and on the same day he considered the possibility of a triangular war [against both England and France]. On Monday morning Monroe, who said he was too busy to undertake the task himself, asked Gallatin to inform Senator Crawford of the two secretaries' wish for a limited war. "I am convinc'd," Monroe wrote, "that it is very important to attempt, at present, the maritime war only. I fear however that difficulty will be experienced in the committee, which may extend itself to the gentlemen, or some of them, at least, at Mrs. Dawsons." The President kept his own counsel.

James Madison did not feel that the times called for any unusual departure from Republican forms, and his deference to Congress was fitting since the war impulse had come from its members rather than the White House. As always, the President left the reading of his message to a clerk who droned it out for almost half an hour. Nor did Madison

directly endorse any particular course. The decision between peace and war, a war "avoiding all connections which might entangle ... [the United States] in the contest or view of other powers" and prosecuted only until an opportunity for peace occurred, "is a solemn question which the Constitution wisely confides to the legislative department of the Government." The President unnecessarily asked "early deliberations" on the question. All he professed to do was to recapitulate the evidence and, in his final paragraph, to suggest that a decision on French relations be postponed until further word came from Barlow. Sometimes Madison was eloquent, sometimes labored and intricate, as when he declared that by impressment "a self-redress is assumed which, if British subjects were wrongfully detained and alone concerned, is that substitution of force for a resort to the responsible sovereign which falls within the definition of war." On the whole, the message compared unfavorably with the annual message presented seven months before.

The President attempted to show that Great Britain was already prosecuting an undeclared war against the United States: "We behold ... on the side of Great Britain a state of war against the United States, and on the side of the United States a state of peace toward Great Britain." Impressment, particularly of native Americans, was an act of war that neither "remonstrances and expostulations" nor friendly offers to regulate the employment of seamen had been able to bring to an end. Indian warriors attacked the West, presumably at Britain's behest. English warships violated American territorial waters. "Pretended blockades," particularly Fox's of 1806, permitted American commerce to be "plundered in every sea." Most important of all, the British Cabinet, "not content with these occasional expedients for laying waste our neutral trade, . . . resorted . . . to a sweeping system of blockades, under the name of orders in council, which has been molded and managed as might best suit its political views, its commercial jealousies, or the avidity of British cruisers." Justified as retaliation, although long since "deprived of this flimsy veil" by French repeal, the Orders in Council and the ancillary license trade were really a war upon American commerce. Economic pressure on the one hand, and, on the other, offers to join Britain if she withdrew her regulations while France remained stubborn, had failed to bring the Cabinet to its senses. "Such," said the President, "is the spectacle of injuries and indignities which have been heaped on our country, and such the crisis which its unexampled forbearance and conciliatory efforts have not been able to avert."

The use of hyperbole did not destroy the essential truth of Madison's indictments of England. In Henry Adams' words, "For five years, the task of finding excuses for peace had been more difficult than that of proving a *casus belli*."[3] That impressment and hovering off American shores had scarcely been mentioned in recent diplomatic correspondence, until the former was pushed to the fore at the very end, proved only that the American government had lost hope of peaceful arrangements, not that the acts were less criminal. The British restrictive system was, as Madison stated, heavily tinctured with selfishness. Had Madison emphasized the harmfulness of the orders, he would have been on more solid ground. To connect their justice with French re-

peal, and to assert in the face of the evidence that French repeal was a fact, simply invited criticism, although the administration's policy since 1810 made emphasis on this theme almost inevitable.

In later years Madison came fairly close to apologizing for his decision to present a war message in June, 1812. "The circumstances under which the war commenced on our part," he wrote in 1813, "require that it should be reviewed with a liberality above the ordinary rules and dispositions indulged in such cases. It had become impossible to avoid or even delay war, at a moment when we were not prepared for it, and when it was certain that effective preparations would not take place, whilst the question of war was undecided." The moment, Madison observed in retrospect, appeared propitious. Napoleon's Grand Army lay poised for an attack on Russia. "Had the French Emperor not been broken down as he was, to a degree at variance with all human probability, and which no human sagacity could anticipate, can it be doubted," the President asked, "that G.B. would have been constrained by her own situation and the demands of her allies, to listen to our reasonable terms of reconciliation." In this spirit James Madison joined the War Hawks. . . .

Madison never firmly controlled the Congress; he often lost command of his own Cabinet; frequently he seemed to drift rather than to direct policy. John Adams, fiercely challenged during the disintegration of Federalism, at least remained firm. In the spring of 1812 the congressional delegate from Mississippi Territory wrote that "the Executive is much censured by all parties for the tardiness of its advances to meet the *tug of war*, and the tenure of Mr. Madison's continuance in the presidential chair, in my opinion, depends upon the success of

3 Henry Adams, *History of the United States During the First Administration of James Madison*, New York, 1890, vol. II, p. 221.

our hostile preparations." Yet the President did not forcefully support the cause of those whose loyalty had to be preserved for the impending election, nor did he speak out in favor of a course that might have maintained the peace he cherished. He reigned but he did not rule. After the declaration of war Jonathan Roberts [Congressman from Pennsylvania] wrote: "The world are pleased to suppose I am on good terms at the White House which by the way is no advantage for the cry of mad dog is not more fatal to its victim than the cry of executive connexion here." Madison won reëlection, but he was the least respected victor the country had yet known.

The war came, not because of the President, but despite him. The war came, not for any single reason, but from the interplay of many. The nation did not want war, and surely it did not embark gleefully on a great crusade. Tired of the self-flagellation and the disgrace that had marked the years since 1805, propelled by the fear of ridicule for inconsistency and by an honest interest in the nation's honor, a sufficient number of congressmen allowed themselves to support war. Justification for a declaration of war was not wanting, and the long-term results were probably beneficial. Still, the war came just when the United States might have enjoyed without a struggle the immense benefits of the neutrality in which so much Christian forbearance (or cowardice) had been invested. Neither side sought the War of 1812, and in the short run it was tragically unnecessary.

GEORGE DANGERFIELD, like Heaton and Horsman
born in Great Britain, now lives in California.
He has written on both English and American history.
In 1952 he won both the Pulitzer and Bancroft
prizes for *The Era of Good Feelings*. Although
primarily a study of the postwar era, this volume
contains an introductory section on the outbreak of
war in 1812 and on the negotiations at Ghent in
1814 that brought it to a close. The following selection
summarizes and evaluates Madison's war message.*

The War Message of June 1, 1812

The so-called War Message, when at
length it was sent to Congress on June 1,
1812, may not rank high in polemical
literature, but it was, as to four fifths of
its contents, a dignified and forcible pre-
sentation of the American case against
Great Britain. It did not go back beyond
the year 1803. It omitted "unrepaired
wrongs of inferior magnitude," though
these might have thronged its pages. It
was content to offer, under five heads, a
series of major British acts hostile to the
United States as an independent and
neutral nation.

"British cruisers," the President began, "have
been in the continued practice of violating
the American flag on the great highway of
nations, and of carrying off persons sailing
under it, not in the exercise of a belligerent
right founded on the law of nations against
an enemy, but of a municipal prerogative
over British subjects. British jurisdiction is
thus extended to neutral vessels in a situation where no laws can operate but the law
of nations and the law of the country to
which the vessels belong.... The practice,
hence, is so far from affecting British subjects alone that, under the pretext of searching for these, thousands of American citizens,
under the safeguard of public law and of
their national flag, have been torn from their
country and from everything dear to them;
have been dragged on board ships of war of
a foreign nation and exposed, under the
severity of their discipline, to be exiled to
the most distant and deadly climes, to risk
their lives in the battles of their oppressors,
and to be the melancholy instruments of
taking away those of their own brethren."

It may well be argued that, in continuing
with the practice of impressing American

*From *The Era of Good Feelings* by George Dangerfield, pp. 21-24, copyright, 1952, by
Harcourt, Brace & World, Inc. and reprinted by permission of the publishers.

seamen after the battle of Trafalgar had made her mistress of the seas, Great Britain had committed not only a crime, which was bad, but an error, which was worse. It is surely impolitic to goad with insults a country with whom it is increasingly to one's interest to stay at peace. It is sufficient to say that had Madison been able to allude, not to "thousands" of impressed Americans, but only to one, he would have had, then and there, his *casus belli.* Great Britain, however, had received no warning that America intended to make war on such a ground; and . . . impressment, though bitterly resented, had up to this point been officially considered as irrelevant to the main issues. It would not have been casuistical in the British had they maintained that, in putting impressment in its rightful place at the head of his list of grievances, Madison had not strengthened his argument but weakened it.

His second complaint was open to the same objection. He went on to say that British cruisers, not content with enforcing their country's municipal law upon an international highway, had violated the rights and peace of the coasts of America. "They hover over and harass our entering and departing commerce. To the most insulting pretensions they have added the most lawless proceedings in our very harbors, and have wantonly spilt American blood within the sanctuary of our territorial jurisdiction." This was irresistibly true: but this, too, strange as it may seem, had never before been advanced as a ground for war.

The President then presented a third grievance which, upon any consideration, was unexceptionable. "Under pretended blockades, without the presence of an adequate force and sometimes without the practicability of applying one, our commerce has been plundered in every sea, the great staples of our country have been cut off from their legitimate interests." To make matters worse, the British had had the hypocrisy to declare "as the true definition of a legal blockade 'that particular ports must be actually invested and previous warning given to vessels bound to them not to enter.' "

Madison had now reached the heart of the matter. His fourth grievance referred to a gross extension of this system of pretended or "paper" blockades. "Not content with these occasional expedients for laying waste our neutral trade, the cabinets of Britain resorted at length to the sweeping system of blockades, under the name of orders in council, which has been molded and managed as might best suit its political views, its commercial jealousies, or the avidity of British cruisers." It was against the unflattering pretensions of these Orders-in-Council, which interdicted the coasts of Europe to American commerce and enforced the interdiction outside the harbor of New York, that Jefferson and Madison had aimed their policy of peaceful coercion. The President now permitted himself a display of bad temper not inappropriate to the complex system of robbery, whose ramifications he proceeded to summarize:

"It has become, indeed, sufficiently certain that the commerce of the United States is to be sacrificed, not as interfering with the belligerent rights of Great Britain; not as supplying the wants of her enemies, which she herself supplies; but as interfering with the monopoly which she covets for her own commerce and navigation. She carries on a war against the lawful commerce of a friend that she may the better carry on a commerce with an enemy — a commerce polluted by the forgeries and perjuries which are for the most part the only passports by which it can 'succeed."

Had the message ended at this point, it would have represented the legitimate complaint of a pacific, unmilitary nation which was being forced into war against its own will because of a gross violation of its neutral rights. Although it is not customary for a people against whom a declaration of war is being urged to read with any sympathy the documents that urge the declaration, it is hard to believe that this part of Mr. Madison's message, when at length it was published in England, was not read without some feelings of shame.

How comfortably, none the less, might such feelings have been put to sleep by the President's recital of his fifth grievance. "In reviewing the conduct of Great Britain towards the United States *our attention is necessarily drawn to the warfare just renewed by the savages on one of our extensive frontiers* — a warfare which is known to spare neither age nor sex and to be distinguished by features particularly shocking to humanity. It is difficult to account for the activity and combinations which have for some time been developing themselves among tribes in constant intercourse with British traders and garrisons without connecting their hostility with that influence and without recollecting the authenticated examples of such interpositions heretofore furnished by the officers and agents of that government."

In these words, Mr. Madison connected the British with that singular chain of events which led to the battle of Tippecanoe. The diffidence of his language suggests the posturing of a man who is about to take a dive into very dangerous waters; and, indeed, the addition of the fifth grievance was not very wise or very helpful. For though the British record in their dealings with the Indians was an unsavory one — though there was nothing fanciful in the Western belief that they would not hesitate to loose upon the frontier all the horrors and miseries of an Indian war; though their innocence in this particular instance was the innocence of people who were not yet ready to be guilty — it is only just to admit that, if they had had their way, there would have been no battle of Tippecanoe at all.

Suggestions for Further Reading

The cause, or causes, of the War of 1812 have interested legions of scholars. The most recent guide to the voluminous literature on the subject is the annotated bibliography in Reginald Horsman, *The Causes of the War of 1812* (Philadelphia, 1962), pp. 269–292. More extensive comments on a smaller number of works are to be found in the masterful but now somewhat dated article by Warren H. Goodman, "The Origins of the War of 1812: A Survey of Changing Interpretations," *Mississippi Valley Historical Review*, vol. XXVIII (1941–1942), pp. 171–186. Also helpful is the standard aid, Samuel F. Bemis and Grace G. Griffin, *Guide to the Diplomatic History of the United States, 1775–1921* (Washington, 1935; New York, 1951), pp. 113–155.

The interested student will wish to read in full the writings excerpted in this volume. Adams, Brant, Burt, Perkins, and Pratt provide relatively full treatments of the chain of events leading to war. So too does Reginald Horsman in the volume cited above. The most complete treatment of the development of British policy, comparatively unstudied by historians, is in Perkins' volume. Albert Z. Carr, *The Coming of War: An Account of the Remarkable Events Leading to the War of 1812* (Garden City, 1960), although based on less intensive research than the other general works, is a lively and sometimes provocative account of the era.

Specialized studies most often concentrate on the problem of war spirit in the West. Horsman's article reviews much of this literature. Early suggestions that fear of the Indians accounts for Western war sentiment are Dice R. Anderson, "The Insurgents of 1811," American Historical Association, *Annual Report for 1911* (Washington, 1913), vol. I, pp. 167–176, and Christopher B. Coleman, "The Ohio Valley in the Preliminaries of the War of 1812," *Mississippi Valley Historical Review*, vol. VII (1920–1921), pp. 39–50. The land hunger argument is sketched in Howard T. Lewis, "A Re-Analysis of the Causes of the War of 1812," *Americana*, vol. VI (1911), pp. 506–516, 577–585. Western imperialism also receives attention in Albert K. Weinberg, *Manifest Destiny* (Baltimore, 1935), a massive compendium, and George Dangerfield, *The Era of Good Feelings* (New York, 1952), a brilliant synthesis. George R. Taylor, "Prices in the Mississippi Valley Preceding the War of 1812," *Journal of Economic and Business History*, vol. III (1930), pp. 148–163, provides statistics supporting the argument put forward in the excerpt in this volume.

British assaults upon American neutral rights dominate the story of the coming of war in Alfred T. Mahan, *Sea Power in Its Relations to the War of 1812* (2 vols.; Boston, 1905), and both British and French attacks are examined in detail in Anna C. Clauder, *American Commerce as Affected by the Wars of the French Revolution and Empire* (Philadelphia, 1932). James F. Zimmerman, *Impressment of American Seamen* (New York, 1925), unfortunately weak on the British side, is the only detailed treatment of the subject. For a British point of view, see Anthony Steel, "More Light on the Chesapeake," *The Mariner's Mirror*, vol. XXXIX (1953), pp. 243–265. Lawrence S. Kaplan, "Jefferson, the Napoleonic Wars and the Balance of Power," *William and Mary Quarterly*, Third Series, vol. XIV (1957), pp. 196–217, is an interesting effort to explain the apparent pro-French bias of Jefferson and his followers.

The great experiment to find an alternative to war is best considered in Louis M. Sears, *Jefferson and the Embargo* (Durham, 1927), although of course the Embargo receives detailed treatment in general studies as well. Irving Brant, *James Madison, Secre-*

tary of State, 1801–1809 (Indianapolis, 1953), discusses and in general approves commercial warfare. Caroline F. Ware, "The Effect of the American Embargo, 1807–1809, on the New England Cotton Industry," *Quarterly Journal of Economics*, vol. LXI (1925–1926), pp. 72–88, challenges the view that the Embargo stimulated American manufacturing. For the impact of American restrictions on the British economy, the interested reader is advised to turn to Eli F. Heckscher, *The Continental System* (London, 1922); François Crouzet, *L'Économie Brittanique et le Blocus Continental* (2 vols.; Paris, 1958); Lowell J. Ragatz, *The Fall of the Planter Class in the British Caribbean* (New York, 1928); and W. Freeman Galpin, *The Grain Supply of England during the Napoleonic Period* (New York, 1925).

Two sympathetic biographical studies, Brant's volume on Madison as President and Bernard Mayo, *Henry Clay, Spokesman of the New West* (Boston, 1937), contain excellent accounts of the war session of 1811–1812. On Madison's role, Theodore C. Smith, "War Guilt in 1812," Massachusetts Historical Society, *Proceedings*, Third Series, vol. LXIV (Boston, 1931), pp. 319–345, is helpful. Alfred B. Sears, *Thomas Worthington, Father of Ohio Statehood* (Columbus, 1958), examines the session from the angle of vision of an anti-war Republican from the West. Federalist grumblings, often amusingly wide distortions of truth, dominate Clarence S. Brigham, ed., "Letters of Abijah Bigelow, Member of Congress, to His Wife, 1810–1815," American Antiquarian Society, *Proceedings*, New Series, vol. XL (Worcester, 1931), pp. 305–406, and George H. Haynes,

ed., "Letters of Samuel Taggart, Representative in Congress, 1805–1814," *ibid.*, vol. XXXIII (Worcester, 1923), pp. 113–226, 297–438. Highly entertaining and informative is the British minister's account published as Richard B. Davis, ed., *Jeffersonian America: Notes on the United States of America . . . by Sir Augustus John Foster, Bart.* (San Marino, 1954). A brilliant account of one of the winter's strangest episodes is Samuel E. Morison, "The Henry-Crillon Affair of 1812," *By Land and By Sea* (New York, 1953), pp. 265–286.

Contemporary materials make clear the depth of emotion at the time. The *Annals of Congress* and *Hansard*, although both incomplete and somewhat unreliable, capture the major arguments. Two British pamphlets, James Stephen, *War in Disguise; Or, the Frauds of the Neutral Flags* (London, 1805), and Alexander Baring, *An Inquiry into the Causes and Consequences of the Orders in Council; and an Examination of the Conduct of Great Britain towards the Neutral Commerce of America* (London, 1808), demonstrate the wide disagreement over the wisdom of Perceval's policy. Stephen is answered in James Madison, *An Examination of the British Doctrine, Which Subjects to Capture a Neutral Trade, Not Open in Time of Peace* (Philadelphia, 1806), reprinted in Gaillard Hunt, ed., *The Writings of James Madison* (9 vols.; New York, 1900–1910), vol. VII, pp. 204–375. Other contemporary American arguments are collected in Matthew Carey, *The Olive Branch, or Faults on Both Sides, Federal and Democratic*, Third Edition; Boston, 1815, and many other printings).